Growing Old Is a Family Affair

*Dorothy Bertolet Fritz*

JOHN KNOX PRESS
ATLANTA

ALSO BY DOROTHY BERTOLET FRITZ

The Spiritual Growth of Children
Activity Programs for Junior Groups
The Use of Symbolism in Christian Education
Primary Teacher's Guide on Spanish Americans
The Child and the Christian Faith
Christian Teaching of Kindergarten Children
Ways of Teaching

Library of Congress Cataloging in Publication Data
Fritz, Dorothy Bertolet.
    Growing old is a family affair.

    Bibliography: p.
    1. Aging. I. Title.
BF724.8.F74 1972   301.43'5   78-37420
ISBN 0-8042-2078-6
Second printing 1976
  John Knox Press 1972
Printed in the United States of America

~§CONTENTS

ᴥ§INTRODUCTION

Why Another Book?

Have you ever come up against the fact that gerontology and geriatrics mean *you?* Very likely these words have not long been in your everyday vocabulary, but suddenly they confront you on every side. If you look in the dictionary you find that gerontology means "the scientific study of the phenomena of old age"; and that geriatrics is "that subdivision of medicine which is concerned with old age and its diseases." But what *is* old age? What are its special phenomena? What are its particular diseases? And where do *you* come in? The definitions sound a bit grim!

I had retired from a job I loved at sixty-five and had just passed my seventieth birthday. The mother and aunt who lived with me were in their nineties. Now, to my surprise, all of us had become part of a serious social problem—perhaps even more serious than that other problem group, "the delinquent adolescent." Today each group seems to constitute a major disaster area for communities, families, and the individuals themselves. And judging from the volume of literature, the many social agencies, and the research groups dealing with what is politely called "later maturity," those who have passed the traditional three score and ten seem to be taking over the headlines.

I had not paid much attention to milestones, but somehow this particular birthday shocked me into a realization of age. I had never really thought of myself as old, elderly, or even middle-aged. Like my mother, who at ninety-six spoke of women twenty years younger as "those old ladies," I had never so categorized myself. For one thing, too many crises, rich experiences, and new opportunities kept popping up for me. There had not yet been a perceptible downhill trend to life. For another, I had always been associated with various age groups (particularly children), and with active, creative, and committed adults.

Suddenly, however, the news from my friends was of retirement plans, of the birth of great-grandchildren in the family, of loved ones in nursing homes, and of death. In our family the generation of my parents was already gone. I had been caring for the "righteous remnant"—two widows and one unmarried aunt —at various times during the last twenty years. And, as I looked back, this was true of many of my friends, with varying degrees of mental, physical, financial, and emotional strain. Apparently many of us are living longer. Some of us are liking it less!

Shock and curiosity then led me to read the newspaper and magazine articles I had been passing by, to notice and think about the people that are more and more my associates, to secure from available libraries some of the books being written about me and my kind.

I was appalled!

In the main they were coldly scientific, even grim. They were full of generalizations. Many of them assumed that one begins to prepare for old age in late middle years and that the most serious difficulties have to do with retirement from a job. Only the more recent writers seemed to be aware of the great variety of *individuals* involved, the widening span of years included, the outdated assumptions—downright myths—that still persist. But surely these older persons are not subjects for detached research and false generalizations that center mainly around illness, indigence, decrepitude, and bad dispositions!

Practically all of my own experience was and is at variance with what I was reading. I had found the older people in our family and circle of friends delightful in many ways. They had the interesting mixture of virtues and faults we find at every age. It would be impossible to generalize about them. From fifty to one hundred years old—or *young!*—they were and are as different in temperament, needs, interests, abilities, financial status, and appearance as those in any other group.

Of course, all elderly people have problems, but so have pre-schoolers. And the younger we are the less wisdom and experience we have to deal with our problems, and the more intensely emotional, and therefore painful, is our reaction to them. Of course, some elderly people are very difficult to deal with. But is this not true of adolescents and young adults? They want what they want when they want it, and can be exceedingly unpleasant when they don't get it. Of course, the aging and aged are often pessimistic and negative. But is this not also true of those in middle age who see the years slipping away with their dreams, ideals, and goals unfulfilled?

And so I thought that there might be within my experiences some useful principles for dealing with problems of aging. In the process of reading in the field of geriatrics, of talking with people young and old, of thinking through personal experiences, such principles began to emerge and take form.

The first of them seemed very clear: *growing old is a family affair*. Attitudes toward aging and the aged, preparation for later years and the actual experiencing of them happen in or are related to families. These attitudes correspond somewhat with three broad periods of life: youth, during which our concepts and characters are formed; middle age, the burden-bearing time; and old age, a lengthening span that can mean dependence or independence, increasing frustrations or rich rewards. It might be helpful to consider the opportunities and problems related to aging in each of these groups, and within the structure of a family.

But we cannot assume that every man or woman marries, has children, and a fairly good job. This, of course, "ain't necessarily so." There are people who at some time in life have no close family ties, who have never had a love of their own. To these can be added large numbers who know desperate poverty or handicapping illness. We are beginning to realize that most of those who are lonely, poor, or physically handicapped are not so through their own fault. Even if they are at fault wholly or in part, they are still as human beings entitled to concern and affection, comfort and healing.

Fortunately there are more and more individuals, agencies, public and private institutions ready to serve such human need. It is not true that all of us shrink from becoming involved in the suffering of others. If we do—which is human also—perhaps we shrink even more from seeing it continue. There are few deep human needs for which there is not somewhere some kind of help, someone who is concerned. The *way* such help is given may at times be lacking in amount and in grace, but it exists, and everyone who needs it is entitled to it.

In my earlier working days I became acquainted with a woman who was badly crippled with arthritis. Her hands were so twisted as to be almost unusable. She managed to care for a small apartment on an income furnished by her two sons, both married and living in other cities, but very affectionately related to her. One was a doctor, the other a college professor. Widowed when her boys were very young, she put aside the modest resources left her for their education. Wanting to be with them during the day she worked at night cleaning offices, after her sons were safely in bed. Surely not only their children, but their country owe such workers a great debt—one that cannot be paid by a barren and inadequate concern for their minimum physical needs. Also it becomes increasingly obvious that the children of parents in such circumstances must somehow be given decent surroundings, health services, and adequate education if cycles of poverty are to be broken.

It is fair to say that this book is oriented largely to our growing middle class. This is deliberate and is related to a second insight: here are the people most apt to buy and read such a book. They are also the people who are in a position to change the whole atmosphere of a culture in a given area. To make such a change successfully—and quickly—cannot be done by the very young or very old and *will* not be done by the very rich or very poor. Those men and women who are parents and between twenty-five and sixty years of age are the ones chiefly responsible for the training of the young and the care of the old. So it seems wise to address this book to their needs and opportunities. However, I hope that young adults, or even adolescents, as well as those of "later maturity" may find something of interest and help in it. The type of family and education described here is not very demanding as far as money is concerned. But it may be demanding in terms of thought, time, and energy. In principle, the suggestions made here can be applied in relatively underprivileged families, in those of more than average income, in institutions and foster homes for youth, and in all the many places where the aged are living.

Before going further, perhaps it would be well to look at a few facts, for many that we have do not agree at all with our commonly accepted ideas about the aging and the aged.

Factual information can do much to dispel such negative myths as, for instance, the myth of *aloneness.* Almost 70 percent of the men and women over 65 are still living as couples, as widowed heads of households, or with relatives. Only 3 to 4 percent live in institutions; 15 to 30 percent live alone—the larger number in this last instance being women.* Up to 70 years of age 89 percent are relatively healthy; less than 1 percent are truly senile; less than 10 percent have hardening of the arteries. The brain continues to develop and be active if *used*.

Other myths relate to finances and to employment. With the increase of life-long savings plans, pensions, and social security, income is less and less a serious problem for the aging, except for those who have long endured poverty, lack of education, or unemployment, or who are physically handicapped. The greatest fear is of long, serious illness. The possibility of some degree or kind of employment constantly expands. It has been discovered that, beyond their accumulated knowledge and skills, these older men and women have a keen sense of loyalty, and that they are stable, responsible, and less prone to industrial accidents, absenteeism, and job shifting. They can bring rich gifts to advisory, part-time, or volunteer positions.

Whether with the passing of time these statistics change or not, the world in which we will live will be different from that of today. In education for aging, the most important principle is to educate for an open, friendly attitude toward *change*. It's bound to come, faster and faster. Why not be ready for it?

*These percentages are not precise but approximate.

PART I *It's Never Too Early*

We are told that at conception we begin to age. It might sound a bit more encouraging to say that at conception we begin to learn and grow. So why not begin at the earliest possible moment—say, babyhood—to get ready for old age? To begin to become the kind of person who will be a satisfaction to himself and everyone around him, no matter how long he lives? It is really never too early to initiate this kind of self-education, or to share it with the children for whom you are responsible.

Of course, this hypothetical baby cannot set goals in his cradle; nor will he lie there thinking of the kind of person he'd like to be at ninety. But much of what happens to him from there on out determines the kind of person he *will* be. So he is fortunate if he has chosen his parents with care! Youth, especially young childhood, is a period of emotional self-centeredness. Babies and young children respond only to those who make them comfortable and happy. This type of response continues to some degree through life, but increasingly, older children turn to those who help them to learn and grow. Adolescents want to achieve, to be liked, to be free persons. Therefore they respond to those who encourage and assist them to grow. Young adults are concerned with finding a vocation and a mate, establishing a home and a family, becoming a citizen. These successive goals are governed largely by emotion. Everything and everybody is measured by their contributions to the desired attainment, by their effect on "Me." They are respected, loved, hated, or viewed with indifference accordingly.

Also, youth lives in the Now. The important things are those which concern the present and the immediate future. It seldom occurs to a young person that the past matters, that it has made him and his world, that he can learn from it much that is of value. He is seldom concerned about his own middle or late maturity, except to be certain it must be of a different or better quality from anything he has yet known. Until this age of continuing wars and atom bombs he had almost never conceded the possibility of death. And even now he does not really believe that his own life might be crippled or ended by accident, illness, or death at any time. His dreams, ambitions, goals tend to be short-range and do not include the prospect of aging.

But the parents, teachers, and employers, the grandparents, uncles, and aunts of these young people are beginning to have glimpses of an inevitable future. The difficulty so far is that most of those called "mature adults" do not really want to look at this future until they stumble over it—and then it is already too late. Somehow the view has been unpleasant. First there is "the empty nest"; the home with children no longer in it. Other interests, other authorities have claimed them—study, work, marriage. Then there is a middle-age fear of being no longer needed as a person. This usually involves facing retirement from the work which has given income and status.

But perhaps the most frightening "view ahead" is of aging —of becoming really *old*. Here is the vision that most of us have had: a stereotype of a person feeble, helpless, broken, needy, ill, irritable. No doubt we too will be white-haired, wrinkled, stooped;

too thin or too fat; unsmiling and harsh-voiced. We will have minds that have ceased to be active, uninterested in new experiences or companions. We will lack a role to play in life, being neither wanted nor needed.

But most of these "views," insofar as they picture the majority of today's very old people, are pure folklore! How many over-sixty persons do *you* know who correspond to all or even a large part of such a description? I suspect we have all been sold a bill of goods by advertisers! Propaganda for youth, for looking young, lovely, and appealing sells billions of dollars worth of cosmetics and services. Even those who are too young to need such aids are conned by these massive campaigns.

And after all, *why?* Youth is far from being the happiest time of life. Everything matters too much, and we have not the wisdom or experience needed to deal with our heartbreaks. Many a boy or girl who suffers over physical defects and unpopularity at sixteen is a person of distinction and delightful to know at sixty.

Chapter 1 PROPAGANDA FOR AGING

There is an East Indian fable about six blind men and an elephant. Never having "seen" an elephant they went together to do so. The first man bumped against the elephant's side and exclaimed, "The elephant is like a wall!" The second meanwhile felt his trunk and insisted, "No, the elephant is like a snake." The third touched the tip of a tusk and was sure the elephant was like a spear. The fourth, putting his arms around a great leg, found him more like a tree. The fifth, grasping a flapping ear, felt a resemblance to a fan. And the sixth, holding the tail was certain the elephant was like a rope. What a quarrel arose over the nature of the elephant!

So it is with our judgments, attitudes, prejudices, values. They are formed largely as a result of our experiences. But they are also to a lesser degree conditioned by what we are taught or told. It may be that our generally negative attitude toward old age is not entirely due to propaganda for youthfulness. It is also common practice in our culture, without intention or realization, to downgrade much that is old. Witches in fairy tales, "badies" in TV plays, people with unyielding social points of view are *old*. Old toys are discarded, old games and amusements are boring, old clothes are out of date and so rejected.

Family Relationships

One of the most common forms of such negative propaganda is quite personal, having to do with family relationships. Parents have a habit of saying, in the hearing of their children, such things as these:

"I won't make my children go to church, as I had to do." Quite ignored is the fact that in the small town in which they lived, everyone was in church. Sunday morning would have been quite lonely on the home street!

Or, "I want you to have advantages. *My* parents wouldn't give me dancing lessons." Or, "You should be glad you have *any* allowance—I never had one. Any spending money *I* had was earned!" Or, "I didn't have *any* clothes of my own. I always had to wear hand-me-downs."

There is no added word to explain that such deprivations were not due to cruel parents, but to the fact that there was little money in those days for anyone. Perhaps our school clothes were possible only because a mother or father went without any new clothes until they had to have them.

It is amazing how carelessly parents make critical comments in the hearing of their children about events, places, and people they really want them to respect or love. For instance, when an elderly relative must become part of a family there may be difficult adjustments to make in the use of space, time, and money. There may even be some facts to face about possible clashes of authority and personality. But the way we discuss such matters can make them sound like an end to joy or like an interesting adventure!

Without being Pollyannas, all families must learn to face such adjustments to older people with courage and humor. If you don't believe it can be done, read John Van Druten's, *I Remember Mama* or Sam Levenson's, *Everything But Money* and other similar books. One of the amusing and endearing qualities of entertainers such as Sam Levenson, Danny Thomas, and Bill Cosby is their affectionately humorous attitude toward their family and community backgrounds. They face the remembered problems and conflicts with compassionate understanding rather than with dislike or distaste. They know that these or similar events are a part of the human condition at every age.

Our negative feelings need not concern a new member of the family. Instead they may precede a necessary visit to an elderly relative or friend. If so, the visit should be given the aura of a "fun" excursion—never, "the poor old man is lonely; we *ought* to go see him!" Whether the visit is to a nursing home or a retirement center, an attractive house or a shabby walk-up flat, it is well to anticipate pleasure, not boredom. If possible have a real *reason* for wanting to see the person involved: pictures to show or to have identified, a question about the family in other days or lands, a good school record to show. Or have a story to tell about the person you are going to see—funny, exciting, relevant, or perhaps of the courage with which they are facing pain or deprivation.

Appearance

For every elderly man and woman who is unnecessarily shabby, out-of-fashion, and poorly groomed, there is another who is a pleasure to see. He or she may be erect, immaculate, charmingly old-fashioned, distinguished, or distinctive. Smart clothes are being designed for older people and our statistics tell us that many can buy them. Of course there are some who—responding to the propaganda for youthfulness—appear with too youthful clothes, too much makeup, and hair that is obviously false or dyed. But there are enough older men and women, especially among motion picture and television greats, who make the kind of chic appearance that is appropriate to their age, to offset the generally negative feeling our society has about old people. Call attention to them!

Abilities

Youth admires competence, ability, achievement. In your family, among your friends, in books, and in all kinds of real-life experiences competent workmen can be found. It does not matter in what area the competence may be. Every child in our town was fascinated by one of the few blacksmith shops still in existence. Besides appearing somewhat dangerous, the skill with which the blacksmith shod ponies and horses and made decorative ironwork for houses greatly impressed them. Never let the interesting hobbies or accomplishments of older people be hidden under a bushel!

Every family and community may have in it those who played exciting parts as pioneers, refugees, seamen. Most families have worked their way out of more than one disaster: dust bowls or depressions, wars or physical handicaps. Biography and history are full of the names of people past middle age who made great contributions to the arts, industry, science, and inventions. Such achievements need not be spectacular. When I was in high school and there was money to be raised, mother and I made sandtarts (thin cookies, crisp and delicious) from my English great-grandmother's recipe. My schoolmates had to stand well with me to be allowed to buy them! It is a matter of sharing any accomplishment that an older person can be proud of and a young one can admire such as baking a super chocolate cake, telling a joke or story, reading palms at a party, or beating everyone in the household at croquet.

Family Memorabilia

Family memorabilia can form the basis for a fascinating bridge over the generation gap. Recently a friend told me of an experience his grown children had in helping to clear the old family home that was to be sold. They made some interesting discoveries: a family Bible with the center record of births, deaths, and marriages; books inscribed as gifts for birthdays, graduations, confirmations; letters related to family crises and romances; picture albums, newspaper clippings, sheet music. These young moderns decided that nothing would do but to ship them all home to make a family scrapbook for *their* children. And who was the most necessary person in this process? The grandmother-in-residence, of course. My own prize find was a box of paperback novels acquired by my grandfather to read on business trips. They were carefully hidden from us in a box in the attic. Oh Grandfather! And nothing is more to be desired for a modern ceremony than an heirloom wedding dress.

Custom and Tradition

Then there is the matter of preserving family customs or traditions. In our country there are always families which are only one generation away from another land or race. When they are escaping from a hated situation they sometimes want to forget all that was left behind. Their children want to become part of their new home as soon as possible. But now we are beginning to discover that beautiful handcrafts, gay folk dances, and a second language can be a very worthwhile heritage from older members of the clan.

Some years ago I was leading a Christmas workshop for church school teachers—a group of busy, tired Christmas-ridden matrons totally uninterested in the whole thing. At last in desperation, I asked "What was the family Christmas custom you loved most as a child?" Backs straightened, eyes shone, hands waved—and we all had a *wonderful* time. Always there had been the same angel or star on the top of the tree, the same crèche or farm scene under it! And such heated discussion as to the proper time and way to sing carols, present gifts, or stuff the turkey. Christmas is the only time I do not envy my Jewish friends their wonderful age-old family ceremonials. And here is where our older friends and relatives can make rich contributions.

One such contribution made by a neighbor and dear friend is a poem she wrote in her late eighties. She had a delightful habit of marking "occasions" in life by what she called jingles. But this expression of a Christmas experience is more than that.

When I was a child on my father's farm
And Christmas time drew near,
I would trudge through the snow to the little store,
Oh, the memory is quite clear
Of the little girl with a quarter to spend
For presents for parents, brother, sister, and friend.

My scarlet mittens and scarlet hood
Were white with glittering snow.
My eyes were shining with eagerness,
My frost-bright cheeks aglow,
As I went gladly hurrying down
To the novelty store in the little town.

And oh the rapture, the sheer delight!
The shop's small windows shone
With beautiful things and there was I
With a quarter all my own.
I searched—and will wonders never cease?
I found five gifts for a nickel apiece.

Such beautiful gifts; and trudging home
Through the winter dusk, I knew
A joy and glowing happiness
That has lasted the long years through.
For something of that far Christmas time
Stayed in my heart and still is mine.

—Jennie Palmeter

What an experience to share with our affluent children!

Every family, hamlet, town, or city has the materials for such propaganda; and the colorful, interesting, attractive older people who can bring it to life. What you want to excite in regard to them is not reverence, but *interest*. Here are human beings in whose lives there have been and are excitement, "happenings," movement, human interest, crises.

Anyone who is twenty now can reasonably expect to live past seventy-two. Does it seem a dismal prospect? I wonder what would happen if we should make a concerted effort to give old age a new image?

Chapter 2 EDUCATION FOR AGING

What Is Senility?

Do you know the meaning of senility? The dictionary says "a state of, pertaining to, or exhibiting the characteristics of old age." Notice that the definition does not say that you have to *be* old to have senile ways. And yet the definition also tends to imply that all or most old people are senile. Statistics say that less than 1 percent of them are *really* senile.

Gelett Burgess, years before our present concern about aging, wrote a book called *Look Eleven Years Younger*. It makes an important point with vividness and clarity, and the photographic illustrations are devastating. Mr. Burgess believes that while there are personal habits that contribute to a certain lack of attractiveness in the aging, they have not usually just begun to exist; they have simply become *evident*. The activity, gaiety, and charm of youth tend to distract attention from such habits. Mr. Burgess calls them "signs of senility" and is sure that they appear at any age from fifteen to fifty—or even in childhood.

If this is true it may explain the fact that husbands and wives *seem* to develop irritating habits after marriage, the kind that "just set me crazy"! The habits were there before, but until they became an everyday affair they went unnoticed, or were covered by a rosy cloak of romance and seemed rather endearing.

Perhaps by facing some of the ways of behaving that make us unattractive to others, we can at the same time overcome them in their earliest stages. Certainly it is too late when we are really old. There have been changes in our bodies, minds, and spirits going on as we mature that contribute to the kind of person we will be. Unfortunately at times they harden and become almost irreversible. My mother was a delightful person to have around in her eighties, and the nurse she had then said to me one day, "A nurse soon learns, Miss Dorothy, that when people have always been nice, they get nicer when they are sick or old. But if they've been mean they get meaner!"

Now let us consider what some of these objectionable ways of behaving are that we label "senile" in the aged, but find in existence all through life. Most of them seem to be physical, outward manifestations. But really they are expressions of thoughtlessness, bad temper, self-centeredness, carelessness.
At least we can provide *good* examples for our children.

Speech

Clear, lucid speech, good diction, and a pleasant voice are invaluable assets all through life. We talk so much! I was impressed particularly by one sentence in President Nixon's inaugural address, "Let's stop shouting at each other!" In our noisy world it seems at times impossible to be heard unless we do shout. But any well-trained teacher knows that when a class becomes noisy, you do not raise your voice—you lower it. Speaking under the noise is what gets the attention you want. And any actor or public speaker knows that to be heard all over the theater or hall you do not shout—you simply talk to the people in the back row; you *think* of them.

Our senility expert, Gelett Burgess, tells us that one of the signs of senility is talking indistinctly: to mumble, hurry, or drawl; to cover the mouth with your hand or turn your head away; to drop your voice at a climax or at the end of a sentence; to make useless and distracting motions.

In family conversations avoid *rambling* in relating an incident. It is never necessary to be lengthy, ponderous, repetitive, given to endless narratives or descriptions. Such errors are common to all—and *boring* to all. Common also to all ages are fruitless arguments, critical remarks, negative reactions to the suggestions of others, a sharp, irritable manner.

If, as you get older, you want to keep your touch with younger people, don't lecture! Raising grandchildren properly is not your business; if you dealt with your own children properly *they* are doing the job. Nobody likes to be lectured at any age. Do not speak of your troubles or difficulties in detail; a listener's interest in other people's troubles, ailments, or mishaps soon lags. Even when you are responding to an inquiry, or to what you know is sincere affection or concern, keep your answer brief. As you become middle-aged or aged refrain from too much talk about the past. Especially do not make adverse comparisons of the present with the past.

There is another important matter concerning communication—not speaking, but listening. Mr. Burgess calls it the "single look" and rates it high in charm. An actor knows that no matter how long a play runs, to give it reality he must listen to the words his fellow actors say as if he had never heard them before—or at least appear to do so. There is indeed a singular charm in a person who pays attention to you, is interested, and responsive. One of the constant refrains in the generation gap on both sides is: "But he never listens to me!" Being a good listener will make you an enjoyable person at any age, and downright popular in old age. There are not many people around these days with time to really listen to a child's chatter, a young person's enthusiasms, or the worries of a parent.

Courtesy

Good manners seem to have gone out of fashion somewhat, but they are still appreciated when we find them. To meet a reasonably well-behaved child, a salesperson who cares what you want, or a well-mannered public servant almost comes as a shock; they surely are a joy. In such matters as courtesy and consideration it is necessary to set a good example and expect it to be followed. This must begin in the home, for it is initially based on our desire to please those we love and who love us. If the small acts of service children and young people do, voluntarily or as part of their family duties, are noticed and appreciated it will be easier to develop such habits. Sharing space fairly in rooms, or while traveling or camping; planning birthday surprises; being quiet while important study or work is in progress—the possibilities are endless, and can be extended to friends and relatives outside the home, to playmates, and to guests.

Courtesy and consideration are areas in which to remember what we have been told by Jean Piaget in his studies of child development: up to the age of eleven very little that is permanent is learned from verbal instruction. The younger the child, the more essential is demonstration by an admired or loved adult.

Personal Habits

A child who grows up in an atmosphere that is clean and orderly but not fussy is not apt to become what is known as "a sloppy old man." Cleanliness and orderliness are good habits to form at any age—and they are quite inexpensive! We do not want to be the type of person who can be described as saying, "Clothes, I'm going downtown. If you want to come along, hang on!" Such people are far too prevalent these days.

There are some unattractive personal habits that should be broken at any age, such as constant sniffling, wriggling the nose, or pulling at one's chin or ear. Nervous movements of any part of the body are quite unappealing. At times, of course, they can be the result of bad health. But part of the "personal habits" area should be a constant check on health. We do not want to develop hypochondriacs, but it only makes sense to begin at an early age to correct congenital defects, to have regular medical examinations, and to take preventive shots.

Responsibility

Perhaps the most important part of education is that which results in the ability to make responsible decisions. Training for this too must begin at a very early age and be steadily expanded. Remembering directions, following orders, keeping promises, are all important. But even more so is the increasing ability to to see needs; to face and attempt to solve problems; and to not be overwhelmed by a sense of failure if a first solution fails; in short, to be *a responsible person.* I saw this happen in an institutional home for children, in which the superintendent considered it part of his work to prepare the boys and girls for normal living when they left home at eighteen. A carefully chosen group of women were asked to act as friendly guides to individual young people in choosing clothes, handling money, and taking part in a wide range of ordinary experiences in homes, churches, and community.

In these and other ways we can educate youth for desirable attitudes toward old age and toward becoming the kind of people that will make aging a rewarding experience for themselves and for those around them. But it is important in such education to avoid being "preachy," self-conscious, heavy-handed. With a little thought and planning it can become a natural part of growing up, largely the product of casual words at the right times and good examples at all times!

Setting Goals

Ambitions, goals, dreams are a normal part of human life. They are made up of satisfactory experiences, contacts with the people we love or admire, observation and learning; they constantly change, expand, are enriched. A child will say, "I'm going to take people their mail, like Daddy"; and he begins the process with old envelopes in a box hung around his neck by a string. During school days a little girl has a teacher she loves or an older brother or sister in the Peace Corps. Her dream is to teach and she begins with a "class" of dolls or playmates.

We all know, however, that our dreams do not always come true. We are limited by the extent of our own basic abilities, by family circumstances and duties, by time and effort we waste in wrong directions. The kind of person we want to be; the kind of life we want for ourselves and a possible family, and where we want to live it; the vocation we choose—all these are major parts of our dreams. Like all dream worlds they vary and shift, retreat into mist or become vivid and bright. But their failure or attainment make all the difference in our evaluation of that life and therefore issue in disappointment or satisfaction at its end.

There are two principles that everyone can put into operation:

Don't give up a dream too readily.

Make the best of what cannot—for the moment—be helped.

Perhaps we should begin very early to teach our children, when facing frustrations, to say, "Isn't there another way?" If we can't go *through* an obstacle we may be able to go around it. A boy who is in leg braces can be the best rooter, ticket collector or equipment keeper his baseball team ever had. A girl who considers herself too unattractive to be popular can be a dancer, tennis player, or cook. She can be charming and kind. The same crippled boy cannot compete in the Olympics, but he might become a sports journalist. Such comparatively small roadblocks can stop you only if you let them.

Becoming a Person

We often dream about what we want to do or achieve, but not so frequently about the kind of *person* we want to be. Even less do we make really serious efforts in that chosen direction. A child's desires about himself are usually short-range and achievable: to have curly hair, to be a good swimmer, to get better grades in math, to tell a joke so it is funny. Later a girl dreams of being tall and slim with beautiful hair. Or a young man sees himself as athletic, debonair, and always ready with the right word.

Good health means good looks, even if every feature isn't perfect. Most parents really try to achieve this for their children, with the help of a clinic or a pediatrician. But it takes some concentrated work and considerable time and effort—and at times self-denial—to keep good health and to achieve good grooming. Cleanliness, care of teeth, care of nails, proper exercise, plenty of drinking water, the proper diet, and sufficient sleep, all form a basis for health and good looks. Taking care of our clothes, no matter how few or inexpensive—keeping them clean, pressed, properly hung instead of piled on the floor, hems up or down to the current length, shoes shined—and learning to buy wisely within a clothes budget, or learning to sew, are useful habits. If begun early in life such habits need not mean constant sacrifice or even conscious decisions. They become as natural as breathing. There is also the extra touch—a flower, a ribbon, the right jewelry, a colorful handkerchief.

But the whole thing isn't really easy. Not one of these demands upon your time *seem* difficult until you face the necessity of meeting them all day and every day, year in and year out. If you want to be healthy and attractive, well-read, competent in some art or craft, responsible and likeable, there is always a better way to use time and energy than the one you may at the moment prefer. However, don't be discouraged if at times you seem to completely fail in this education for aging, with yourselves *and* your children. You are human and fallible—but at least you will know you tried!

Many a son or daughter has missed a good marriage or a good job because he or she permitted a demanding and selfish mother or some other family member to stand in his or her way. It is possible to be a coward or a self-made martyr in such instances. The hardest obstacles to overcome are those we have put in our own way. But at least we can try to face our mistakes honestly and not shift the blame to circumstances or other people We do not improve our own lot by living in the shadow of what might have been.

There is nothing more unbecoming to old age than bitterness, nothing that is apt to make an aging person more unhappy or unpopular. In the years between youth and old age we can work with determination to right injustices that have hurt us, to create more favorable opportunities for a new generation, to attain some small measure of what we had hoped for. But bitterness will not only alienate us from such possible gains, but will prove very unpalatable to ourselves and to those around us.

Psychologists tell us that no life is adequate or happy until there is a center for that life, a core by which all experiences are judged and all purposes formed. They go on to say further that, although a life can be *strong* with an unworthy core, it cannot be happy, unless its direction is worthy. A great many people today are beginning to identify this important center for life as *love*—hippies for instance! Unfortunately they are not always clear about the source of love, the meaning of love, or worthwhile ways to express love. Most religions have in them these elements of upward-reaching growth and compassion. Unfortunately these noble sentiments do not always get put into practice! The sooner we decide what life means to us, what we want to do with it, and how we want to live it, the better off we will be. For then we will be in a position to share with our children what we believe in, what to us is truth.

This can be done both in words and deeds. It does not mean that they will or must accept the same beliefs, the same truths. But they are right in resenting the fact that we very seldom share with them our deepest values, acknowledge to them our failures in attaining our goals; or ask their interest, help, and advice—and perhaps their judgment—concerning them.

So we come in the process of growing old to the end of the first life period, including childhood, adolescence, young adulthood. After this—or perhaps earlier—each child will be a mature person, absolutely on his own. What habits he has failed to establish, what lessons he did not learn, what values and goals he did not set are increasingly out of reach. And this just as the most responsible, demanding, difficult part of life is just ahead.

Is he—are you—ready for it?

PART II *It's Almost Too Much!*

One summer during a brief teaching assignment it was necessary to drive to and from the school daily, a twenty-five minute trip. My driver was an elderly man who, with his wife, was giving volunteer service in a church study center. He was very courteous and friendly. As we chatted he told me that he was born into a large family on a small Arkansas farm. "We didn't know we were poor," he said. "We had clothes such as they were, plenty of food, and quite a bit of fun—singing, dancing, swimming, fishing. We all had chores to do and a pretty good basic schooling. Everyone we knew lived the same way. When boys were about fifteen they lit out to look for a job and support themselves. That's when we found out we were poor!"

As I planned the three divisions of this book I remembered this conversation. The memory brought a bit of a shock! Here was a boy expected to be on his own at fifteen and I was classifying youth as continuing on to thirty. But many of our assumptions have changed since his childhood days. School is practically compulsory to the twelfth grade or until the age of eighteen. If anyone "drops out" every effort is made to get him back. Youth Corps, Job Training or two years at a local junior college or vocational school is more and more the rule, any one of which extends the school period so that the student is about twenty when he finishes.

Students who can get scholarships or help from their parents go on through college. Many work for advanced degrees or in various types of internship positions and don't finish school until they are twenty-five or twenty-six. Somewhere before, after, or in between comes a period of military service, or a pause to replenish funds by part-time or full-time work. Somewhere there also comes a time when a young man and girl decide they can no longer put off marriage. If so they may still need help.

Rather than being independent at fifteen, our present-day lad is still somewhat dependent on family or the state at thirty. Let's face it—the most burdened people in history (other than slaves!) in the years ahead are going to be those between twenty-five and sixty-five with established families and jobs. They will continue to help their children through a longer period of education and an early marriage that may be simultaneous with it. They will also bear a tremendous tax burden. There will be an increasing number of elderly people for whom they will be responsible both personally and as citizens. On them, too, will fall the main weight of support of the volunteer services which demand both time and money; and the calls into state and federal government assignments that result in a loss of productive years and income. If these middle-agers are church related, much is expected of them in that area also.

The average citizen of this age and belonging to the middle or upper middle class has or soon will have more than he can bear. This happens just as time for them begins to accelerate and during a period in which they should be making increased preparation for their own later years. Will they be able to make it? Is there any help they can or will have?

Chapter 3 RESPONSIBILITY PLUS

Life between the ages of twenty-five and sixty-five is marked by tremendous pressures from every direction. Demands are made upon the middle-aged by the young, the old, the world of industry, the state, the church. Does this mean, as our young people are insisting, that these people of middle age tend to become production machines—*things*? There seems to be little time and energy left for a continuous life of the spirit; for culture, creativity, varied recreation, religion. At present, it seems that to attain such time means a constant struggle.

If we lack the wisdom, strength, and ability to cope with the situation, the whole system falls apart at some point and life becomes drudgery, permeated with a sense of failure. What are some of the ways we can help ourselves, while society is finding a solution?

Here are a few suggestions.

Saving Money

A successful old age may depend upon a degree of thrift when younger. Of course there are people who can barely *live*, let alone save any great amount of money. But even a person living alone on a yearly income of less than a thousand dollars often has a hiding place for odd pennies and nickels and an idea for their eventual use. It is the *habit* of regular saving that matters. In these days of credit buying it hardly makes sense—nor is it safe—to pay cash for everything. But it still makes very good sense to buy no more than you can pay for immediately upon receiving the bills.

In my faith stewardship is stressed. We believe that since all good gifts are from God, they are to be used in accordance with his will. Natural resources are to be conserved, time and talents to be developed and used, not wasted. Money is to be earned honestly and balanced between what is spent, given, and saved. In accordance with circumstances the balance may shift, but only as is necessary, or as increased income permits a change upward. This seems reasonable to me as a plan for one's own best interests, quite apart from any religious faith. A certain amount of saving is desirable unless we want at some point to give up all responsibility for our lives. Obviously some method of extensive saving must begin at the earliest possible date, through such means as mutual fund savings, investments made through a payroll plan or insurance. It is possible to save a great deal by avoiding installment buying except where absolutely necessary. The interest on such payments can add up to shocking amounts. The exception could be in paying for a home, which today is almost a necessity. Safety demands some type of insurance in the low-earning, high-spending time of early family life. The range of price, type, and coverage is very wide. Insurance on a very young child can be purchased at a low rate and paid out when most needed for education, marriage, or buying into a business.

If you are parents with children to educate, know well in advance what sources for scholarships or educational loans are available and what their conditions are. There are endless numbers of them today, as well as schools with ways of providing work-study plans. Careful planning ahead is necessary also for tax payments, for unexpected family illnesses, and other responsibilities that come along at awkward moments. If you have avoided spending beyond your income, have paid bills promptly, and have a modest saving plan, any reputable bank will give you credit and help you over a bad bump.

Taxes and Citizenship

In the past, we have tended to accept death and taxes as inevitable. As I write this many legislators are uneasily expecting a taxpayer's revolt, and it is probably long overdue. In our country, however, the average citizen pays little attention to tax laws and seldom attends even local hearings, unless he is personally very deeply involved. There has come to be a complex tax system, full of inequities and overlapping, and inadequate to meet the demands made for services. What seems to be needed is a majority combination of legislators and citizens willing to put aside special interests, lobbying, and just plain greed long enough to put into action some of the intelligent studies, reports, and suggestions that have already been made.

This does not mean cutting taxes blindly. It does mean helping to decide priorities for spending (such as education), seeing that prejudices are not perpetuated in our tax structure, and most of all, making sure that unprincipled and powerful men, agencies, corporations, and organizations do not get away with murder! It probably also means paying closer attention to the quality of the men we elect to public office and then not pressuring them into dishonesty by our demands. This type of citizenship is clearly a responsibility of older youth and middle age.

Any city councilman or school board member who is honest and dedicated is grateful for citizens interested enough to attend decisive meetings. Any political party welcomes those willing to give an occasional hour to ring doorbells or get out mail. Much social service comes our way through organizations to which we belong such as lodges, P.T.A., Scouts, A.A.U.W. The teen-age girls known as candy stripers not only serve most acceptably in hospitals but often become therapists, doctors, or nurses. Many a famous man has started his public life as a page in state or national legislatures. In giving service of any kind the interests and knowledge of you and your children are broadened. You make friends with all kinds of people and often open doors to vocational opportunities that might otherwise never have come your way.

Cooperative Living

The word "cooperative" is one that somehow helps to keep life in the hands of individuals rather than the state or huge corporations. Some unions are beginning to fail at this point, as they become more and more governed from the top. Cooperatives can be as small as we want to make them and as personal. Where funds do not permit enough Head Start groups, similar plans are being carried on by mothers and other volunteers. Play groups (a dozen children in a neighborhood) again are staffed by one or two mothers in turn. This covers a period from early morning to noon, omitting meal and nap times, and giving each mother a few hours once or twice a week for shopping or other uninterrupted activities. Such types of work-sharing also lower the sitter budget.

Another form of "cooperative" is the growing number of mothers used as teacher-assistants in under-staffed schools. They take many routine duties and even some supervised teaching tasks from the over-burdened professional teacher. At the same time, acting in this capacity gives mothers an exciting view of the new educational methods being used with their children and some extra funds for themselves. This process also opens to the assistant the possibility of a return to school for additional training for professional teaching. It may mean that the man of the family will choose between jobs on a basis of local educational opportunities for his wife as well as his children. This would be especially true if she interrupted her own education to help him finish school. Practically all the women secretaries and clerks on the staff on which I worked were putting someone through school—sons, daughters, or husbands. When I interviewed nurses to care for my aunt and mother, many of them were going back to work to accumulate first year college funds for a daughter or son about to graduate from high school.

Youth Can Help

Children can begin to work also, mostly with such neighborhood jobs as baby-sitting, running errands, or delivering papers. Decisions must be made here as to which take priority—studies, health, working conditions, or the money earned. Also there is the matter of training in making a budget by deciding how much money to spend, save, or give. Young people nowadays sometimes make almost as much in part-time work as we elders did in our first full-time jobs. It is not easy to face the ethical problems that arise when a sixteen year old with a mediocre voice makes a hit record with electronic help, or when a singing group has a schedule that is too demanding or features suggestive songs.

Children and young people can also begin at a very early age to understand the need for community volunteer services and to take part in them. One way to help is to free mother from household tasks which they can take over, so she will have time to work in the volunteer services. But youth can go far beyond such secondhand efforts. The local hospital in our town could hardly get along without its teen-age girls—the candy stripers mentioned before. Also a boys' club has long been helping to upgrade a badly rundown neighborhood. They supply materials and their own labor to improve housing. They, with the family, add needed rooms, put in solid frames for new windows and doors, plan landscaping and even do work on interior plumbing and electricity with professional supervision.

Both groups are quite proud of their status as useful citizens and act with real wisdom as members of the supervising welfare committees.

"Singles" Can Help

We have been considering the problems of middle age largely in connection with couples who have children. There will also be, in these productive years, men and women living alone —those who are divorced, widowed, or have never married. They will not have the huge expense in the field of educating children, or the time-consuming business of child nurture that parents have, but they will be hit hardest with taxes. Those who build successful careers are often willing to help financially with the school expenses of nieces or nephews. Others, widowed or divorced, may still have responsibility for children of their own, as well as complex emotional difficulties. The unmarried brother or sister in a family is often left to care for sick or aging parents, or becomes a source for loans which somehow never get paid back.

This is not fair. Everyone has a right to insist on some system of sharing responsibilities without being "taken." But there is an area in which the "unmarrieds" can often do a great deal more than they have usually been asked to do—in church, social welfare, and citizenship tasks. Here time, talent, and money are constantly needed.

Canada once had an organization called "Aunts, Inc."—

unmarried working women who gave occasional hours of baby-sitting to harried young parents. One of the most successful kindergarten teachers in a church school was a bachelor of twenty-eight. He says it proved valuable training when he became the father of three.

The Aging Can Help

We have seen briefly what youth and "singles" can do to help hard-pressed parents. Another source of help in volunteer services can be found in the aging. After sixty they still have the abilities and talents, experience and judgment that the years have given them. Think of the potential "drop-outs" they can tutor; the struggling young housewives they can introduce into the secrets of good cooking and budget-and-baby managing! Ex-auditors and math teachers make wonderful treasurers for volunteer agencies. There is actually no knowledge, training, or area of interest that cannot be useful, in services that *must* be volunteer, since there is no money to pay for them. Every agency under every United Fund is desperate for dependable volunteer workers, for whatever time can be spared. Any older person who can navigate and some that can't are needed. One of the outstanding successes of recent years (this one-with a small payment attached) is "Grandparents, Inc." This organization connects an older man or woman with a child in an institution who needs the time, attention, and love of an adult for a few hours daily or weekly.

In the Church

Both the young and old could take over some of the responsibilities in churches and other religious organizations that far too often are given to those in the thirty to sixty age bracket. Older children and youth can serve at meals, keep supplies in order, do

Chapter 4 CAN THIS BE PARADISE?

If you are in the middle-age group, for some years you have been paying a high price for the privilege—in money, time, energy, emotion. Now there is an opportunity to get some of your own back!

When life moves along normally, this is the time when a working man or woman is at the peak of income, prestige, and personal satisfaction. One by one the children have moved out of the home, to school, work, marriage. Statistically a couple will probably have at least fifteen years together after the last child has left the home. Instead of an empty nest syndrome, there can be a second honeymoon, a long one—a few years of near-paradise.

Are you ready for it? Have you become friends as well as lovers? Are you able to talk to one another, not only about personal and family affairs, but about a wide range of other subjects? Have you retained some individuality, instead of merging wholly into parenthood?

Untying Apron Strings

If your children are working, expect them to pay their way, whether in your home or out of it. If they are in school, assume that matters of grades and behavior now will center in the college or university. Do not rush to protect them from self-made trou-

many kinds of office work, deliver flowers and books to the elderly or ill. There is no end to the ways in which the advice and friendly interest of retired people can be used—it is necessary only to be careful not to go beyond a possibly lessened stamina. For the young, middle-aged, and aging, service given to the church of your faith is not only useful, but your own life will be broadened, deepened, and enriched thereby.

For those who have large incomes, giving time and money to volunteer services presents no problem. But with most of us giving time, energy, *or* money can mean very real sacrifice. If such giving can be spread over a broader base, it will not mean the burden it sometimes does to the parents or others of the middle years. In any event, as you take your place in the areas we have been considering you will find life opening up instead of closing in. The new interests you discover and the friends you make will be a rich resource as you go into the period of aging. It need not be a cold plunge!

Nor need it be as an Irish bookie at the Saratoga racetrack suggested years ago. He was taking bets on a pad and having left his glasses at home, could not read his own writing. Looking up with a twinkle in his eyes and a brogue I cannot reproduce he said, "Ain't it fierce? Just about the time you learn how to live you start falling to pieces!"

bles. If they marry, see that the new home is a fully responsible one. The exception to this is the growing trend for parents who are able to do so to make some financial contribution to a couple still in school. This is not a new idea. All through the ages parents have contributed to a new home by a dowry, accumulated household equipment, farm animals, land, a house. If you have not nurtured your children into reasonably responsible adults, it is too late to do so now. They will have to learn the hard way, from people who do not care how much they are hurt. While being interested, loving, and kind, do not become a loan office, a marriage counselor (especially with sympathies all in one direction), or a semiprofessional baby-sitter. It sounds drastic, but it may be best to sell that big house and move into a small one, an apartment, or even a trailer, where there is no room for company.

Young people who are away at school, or at work, or married are no longer apt to be near home. They may be any place in the world. They should be giving the major part of their attention to their studies, new jobs, or families.

Would it not be wise to at times be an honored guest on campus, or in the city where a son or daughter works or is settled in a home of his or her own, rather than to be the person they visit? Young people living on campus or in an apartment prefer not to leave their new friends or activities for any length of time. A newly married couple finds it difficult to decide which in-laws to visit; and if there are young children, vast amounts of luggage are needed. Later, as the family grows, travel to any distance becomes quite expensive and children usually dislike it. Why not go where they are; stay a limited length of time specified in advance; and—horrors!—stay in a motel or hotel instead of making all kinds of trouble about sleeping arrangements.

You'll be very popular if you accept invitations to join your "children" at convenient moments, give them time for their own affairs, and invite them and their friends as your guests on some enjoyable excursions. Goodbye gifts are better than those you bring with you for several reasons, but mainly because by the time you leave you will know what everyone really wants.

Beginning to Be Yourself

Are there many plans that through the years you have made and put aside? Now is the time to resurrect them. You will still be limited in time and perhaps in funds but you can begin to savor some of the joys of retirement by doing what you really want to do in the time you have. A dancing class? a card club? a small boat of your own? short trips around the state? a super garden? At least make a move in the right direction. Dance in your living room to an old familiar record—"our song." Start a special bank account for that boat. Study seed catalogs all winter, or get to work on that outside space if you are fortunate enough to live in a year-round garden climate. Take a one day or weekend trip to the nearest lake or mountain. The point is to get in motion toward those resurrected plans. Make some new ones too—at least one really glamorous vacation trip for instance. Now that you have a little more time and money to spend, *spend them.* And on yourselves, not on your children.

Retirement

If you are a part of the paid labor force of the nation—as most women as well as men will be in the not too distant future —you should begin to think about retirement. Hopefully you have already done so, although far too many employed people leave such considerations to the last minute. How about retirement income? Have you a part in a pension system? in Social

Security? Have you added some kind of personal savings to such income or can you do so now? Can you count on earnings after retirement, by activating an avocation or a type of work for which you have previously had some training or experience? Much depends upon your personal attitude toward your job. If it tends to be your whole life, take time now to gradually decrease your dependence upon it. If it has been just a way to earn a living, begin to think of a put-aside dream that might now become a reality; at least begin to become involved in it. If work has been to you a refuge from home problems, face this honestly and consider what can be done about them. A man might even decide to take over as housekeeper; some men enjoy this. Let your wife try her hand at some work outside the home she has always wanted to do or return to.

At least you have a freedom of choice you perhaps never enjoyed before. You may get real joy from a type of creative work that adds nothing to your income, or offer a service to others not previously possible. In so doing you will find a place in life that has meaning, that brings you new friends, and in which you will learn and grow. Perhaps like many aging people you will find a new and lucrative career. One of the great joys of retirement is to work if you want to, when you want to, and at what you want to!

Health

As the consciousness of growing old is forced upon you, give some attention to your health of mind and body. If you have not had regular physical checkups, get one now and keep on doing so at intervals. Too many colds may indicate a need for special vitamins. Take care of your teeth, eyes, feet, and ears. Some of the national organizations for cancer, tuberculosis, and various diseases of the heart and circulatory system provide tests, free or at low cost. Take them. Take advantage of the services of Medicare. You have helped pay for such programs directly or indirectly. Now they are rightfully yours.

As part of mental health again review your own attitude toward aging. You may be avoiding contact with older relatives or feeling resentful toward them because they are a reminder of your own future. If you seem to be outliving other relatives and your children are scattered, you may feel a sense of isolation or the absence of a protection on which you have counted. This is especially true if there has been a loss of husband or wife by divorce or death. There may be a growing fear of dependence, illness, or loss of status or power. All of these are apt to be illusions and can be dealt with. Women often face such feelings at menopause together with a fear of the loss of vital sexual relationships. Men face the same problem at a different time and in a different way. These fears are largely psychological and can be faced in a spirit of "this too will pass," or with the help of your spiritual advisor, doctor, or psychiatrist.

The real mental health problem now is to keep the mind active and open. Never stop reading, learning, thinking, listening for a moment. Never let yourself develop the kind of rigidity that closes your mind to new ideas and experiences. If you finally reject them, do so for a reason, not just because they are new or different from those in your own background. After all, the context of life changes. For instance, think how space exploration has changed the world, even to our vocabularies. Therefore that world must be considered and acted upon differently. We must welcome this as natural and exciting and train ourselves and our children to accept ever accelerating change.

Remember, since you were thirty *time* has been accelerating.

It will go even faster as you move into the period of aging. You do not want to lose a joyous minute of it.

Spiritual Values

Little has been said so far about spiritual values in life, except to suggest sharing what you have with your children. In our country, such values may range through a variety of humanist-existentialist views, to no end of formal religions. There are many people who refuse to accept the existence of spiritual values. They profess that all human development is purely biological, and that the highest motivation for what is accepted as "good" conduct is enlightened self-interest.

Those of us who profess the Christian faith have long had a questionable habit of labeling all spiritual values and virtuous acts as "Christian" or, at least, as "religious." But it is obvious that many people who adhere to other faiths or who have no religious adherence at all, have nevertheless found motivations for courage, compassion, brotherhood, sacrificial love, and a long list of other "good" values. Many of us have built an odd hodgepodge of beliefs about where man came from, what he is supposed to be doing, and where he will eventually go. Our answers to these questions form the foundation for our value systems, whether we are conscious of them or not. They are built from reality (experience, our existential life) and from what we *accept* of our heritage of knowledge as tested by that experience.

If we accept the dictum of psychologists that a life can be strong only when it has a value system rooted in a core, the necessity of some kind of basic belief about life becomes clear. So does the necessity of testing our values, decisions, and choices by that belief. Even if we do not believe in any kind of divine being, we often come to the point at which we can only say, "From existing evidence I believe . . ." or "This is my basic assumption (or working hypothesis)."

The word "spiritual" as opposed to "carnal" has nothing really to do with religion but indicates a *level* of life—physical, mental, spiritual—that increases in determinative power in that order. If a man sees a dog drowning, and he himself cannot swim, his *body* would say, "Don't risk your life"; his *mind*, "A dog is not worth the risk"; but often something other than either forces him to try to save the dog. The third level has an essence of its own about which we know very little and which we seldom use.

But now—any time after thirty—it is good to take stock of oneself. What kind of a man am I? What is my control center —if I have one? What do I believe about man? about life? What has my life in word and deed said to my children? to others? Perhaps we have never consciously answered these questions. Perhaps we have done so *unconsciously* in late childhood or early adolescence, which is entirely possible. A slum child, for instance, may see a local gangster as a hero, the one who has all the glamorous, desirable possessions—power over others, a seeming invincibility in regard to law. So, deep within himself, he decides that this is the only way to get what he wants in life.

Whether we have a core of values for life is something that it is well to face honestly *now*. If not, life will continue to be a series of scattered and often conflicting decisions and choices made over and over, bringing no serenity or satisfaction. We must listen, read, and think. Then from the results of such honest efforts, we must build our own firm system of values, soundly rooted in a basic attitude toward life. It can be based on both reality and idealism. It may or may not be religious. But we must have one, and it must be our own, not a lazy acceptance of a secondhand one. Probably, like finger prints, there are no two life cores, no two value systems exactly alike.

We are helped, however, by those values which man has come to accept as useful, practical, and satisfying—whatever their source. They include honesty and integrity, intelligent courage and self-sacrifice, learning and wisdom, kindness and love. Have we lived according to these values as best we might in our families, at work and play, as citizens of our own land and of the world?

Even if you do not accept the Bible as your basic guide, it will not hurt you to read Paul's Letter to the Galatians, chapter 5, verses 18–23; and to the Ephesians, chapter 4, verses 23–32. Paul, of course, was referring to the indwelling Spirit of God, who brings guidance and strength. But "spirit" in a secular sense can say just about the same thing to the highest type of thinking man. If I choose to believe that all such guidance, whatever its immediate source, is God speaking in a different way to different needs and understandings, who can prove I am wrong?

In any event, this is a good time to examine your spiritual life. Look for help if it seems a bit anemic, and then work to strengthen it.

A healthy, active mind and spirit in a healthy body is excellent equipment for aging!

Chapter 5 A COLD PLUNGE

Did you ever see a performance of one of the groups of swimmers—sometimes called "Polar Bears"—who take pride in plunging into very cold water in midwinter? Or, to be a trifle more moderate, have *you* ever gone swimming in the cold water along the coast of Maine? Or have you been addicted to cold showers in your own bathroom?

We hope you do not consider the next period of life as a series of such icy experiences, as some people do at this point. They need not be so. If you have been gradually preparing for a series of major changes in life then you will find these changes challenging, stimulating, exciting. And excitement warms the blood! Even retirement, loss of regular occupation, lessened income, and a host of related problems will keep you too busy to feel the cold.

Face it all with courage and common sense. Decide what helpful measures you can take in each area—if you have not already done so. Consider well the warnings given here. And go into all the adjustments to be made with vim, vigor, and vitality. For instance, there is a decision to make as to what your place and way of living will be. You may have already secured part-time work for pay, and if it is entirely different from your previous occupation, it may be as fearful an experience as your first job, years and years ago. I had, up to retirement, faced income tax time quite calmly and filled out the papers myself. After retirement it was much more complicated; there were more records to keep and I had to do it without help. There will be many such changes, some of them quite unexpected.

If you are a wife and housekeeper you may suddenly find that it is not always pure joy to have an unemployed man on your hands. Many a woman has wept on my shoulder that having her retired husband constantly at home is driving her crazy! Part of this may be an unrecognized and unacknowledged resentment of the fact that the man of the house has retired but she has not. If, as a couple, they continue to live as before, she has as much or more to do. Lacking occupation, her husband tends to expect attention and companionship. He also finds more to criticize! Understanding this a wise man will, before actual retirement, take the lead in suggesting simplification of living, especially housekeeping. If his wife is sentimental about her home, or wants to "keep it available for the children" there are a few magic phrases that will weaken her defenses.

"But I want you with me."

"I want to do things together."

"I need you now—while we are still together."

Also, the retiree should already have developed some new personal interests and activities. The possibilities are numerous, dependent mainly upon what you want to learn that you have never learned, what you want to do that you have never done. Some of these experiences can be mutual. For instance, if you are planning to travel, why not learn a new language together? If no classes are available, good records are. Even if you are continuing in a new vocation part- or full-time, all of your future interests should not be vocational. Some of them should lead you into new paths of recreation and culture.

In every way the working person, married or not, should plan to cushion what has been called "retirement shock." Even if you do this, you cannot avoid a sharp realization of the sadder facts of aging—the loss of loved ones, the fact of death, possible failing health, changing life patterns that you dislike. If you have grown up in the kind of ideal family pictured in Part I, even these facts will not throw you off balance. You will find a new sense of achievement in meeting the challenges and problems that come with aging.

New Places and People

Another cold plunge may be into a strange environment. Part of this has to do with people. This includes both leaving those you know and feeling comfortable with and getting to know unfamiliar ones—in new work, a different neighborhood, church, town, or part of the country, where the climate and customs make adjustments difficult. When I was a child my father's work made it necessary to move frequently—so frequently that I was sometimes in boarding school, sometimes in a different town every school year. All children dislike and, at times, fear moving. "Will they like me, Mother?" is the cry. When new playmates failed to take me in immediately, and I wailed about it, Mother would say, "But you know, they got along very well before we came. *You* must be the friendly one."

This latent fear often persists into adulthood. If we do not admit and overcome it, *we* may be the ones to hang back, to seem stiff and unfriendly. *We* may be responsible for our own delay in finding a place among these new co-workers or neighbors. One need not be "pushy." Even a smile, a question, or a request for some minor assistance can open the way for a person who is also shy but quite ready to be welcoming.

The coldness of this plunge may be related to what you are

giving up: work that you loved; a home saturated with pleasant memories; people who were comrades in hobbies, recreation, and service activities; a place in which everyone knew you by name and respected you as a fellow citizen. Admittedly it will take a long time to rebuild a similar framework for life elsewhere; perhaps you will never do so completely. Certainly it cannot happen as long as you don't get at it without the backward looks of Lot's wife.

A most important thing to remember here is not to compare your new location unfavorably with your former home, at least not out loud. Old residents may gripe about obvious disadvantages, but not *new* residents—even if what they say is true. If you cannot stand the apartment, the town, the retirement center, move away. But if you want to be remembered pleasantly, blame it on a height phobia, a desire to be near your grandchildren, your health—on anything but the place.

If you have chosen to move where some of your married children are living, do not depend on them to make a place for you, or make you a part of all their activities. Seek friends of your own and then invite the family to meet your friends. Join organizations with which they are not connected. Use a different supermarket; perhaps even attend a different church. Make your meetings *occasions*, not merely routine or dutiful.

Loss of Loved Ones

If you are married you may at some time in this period face a very cold plunge indeed—the loss of your husband or wife. Statistics tell us it is apt to be the husband who dies first. Perhaps this is part of God's compassion, for it is usually harder for a man to live happily alone than a woman. One thing that should be avoided is promises to each other concerning the future—any kind of promises. In these fast moving days it is hard to tell what the future will bring and it should not be circumscribed. A man often remarries quickly. This does not necessarily mean that he has forgotten his love for his first wife. Usually it means that his marriage was so satisfactory that he finds it impossible to live happily and comfortably alone. Probably he can make some elderly spinster or widow quite happy.

Because she is more self-sufficient a woman is less apt to marry again. The warning needed for her is not to choose some other member of her family or some friend, male or female, as a substitute for her husband. If she does this it means making the most unreasonable demands upon such a person for services and companionship.

It may sound a bit cold, but in fact one of the *warmest* things you can do for your loved ones is to have your affairs completely in order so that when death comes, all necessary legal and business affairs will make as little trouble as possible. There should be complete openness at this point between husband and wife, parents and children. Make clear in writing, and preferably in a will, how and where you want to be buried, what disposal you wish to make of personal or family possessions, where all important records can be found. It is a heartbreaking and sometimes expensive business to have to deal with such matters in a time of great sadness, without proper information.

Loss of Income

Still another "coldness" in which you may find yourself immersed is in connection with money. If you have a large personal income from insurance, investments, or savings; if you do well-paid creative work that can continue indefinitely, there is no problem. If you are living on a pension that is a fractional part of what you formerly earned, extended only by Social Security and the help of Medicare, there may be difficulties. The reduction of income is hampering. You have to make and stay within a reduced budget and do without many pleasures and possessions you had come to take for granted. The records and reports, rules and restrictions with which you become involved make you feel like a subject for welfare. This becomes even worse if it is necessary to accept help from your children in some form.

But try to think clearly. A pension and Social Security are not gifts. You or your spouse have paid for them in work, in contributed funds, in direct and indirect taxes, perhaps to a greater amount than you will ever receive. And as to necessary contributions from your children or from others—friends, relatives, the church, lodges—remember that they come to you because of loving concern. As far as your children enter the picture, they are paying a very small part of a very big debt in both services and money. Organizations and institutions were created for such purposes and are committed to them.

An Empty Place

At least a dash of cold water comes with the feeling that there is no longer a real place in the world for you, that you are no longer needed. But this need not be true. There are endless services to be performed to which your time and talents can be given. Every service agency needs the help of many volunteers— to raise money or to do the many small and large jobs that take the place of money. Let me see if I can mention a number of things that friends of mine who are over seventy are doing:

1. Leading a children's choir, a bell choir, or giving individual vocal lessons.
2. Tutoring school children who are dropping behind.

3. Helping in a hospital: receptionist, saleswoman in the gift shop, etc.
4. Doing research (identifying artifacts) in a museum.
5. Arranging hospitality and excursions for visitors from foreign lands (our town has a great many).
6. Helping in a church organization that supplies hot meals for people who live alone and are elderly or ill.
7. Doing bookkeeping or routine office jobs for volunteer organizations.
8. Keeping an address list up to date for volunteer organizations, to be used in the annual appeal for funds.
9. Volunteer "baby-sitting" with the very young or very old and even in their own family at times!
10. Acting as a friendly counselor to young people who are away from their own families and new to homemaking and parenthood.
11. Teaching the neighborhood boys to use tools.
12. Chatting each day in person or by phone with people who live alone and are elderly or ill.

Every one of these activities fills a real need and can be increased in both quality and quantity to any extent your strength permits. If you cannot serve but have reached a point at which you must be wholly served, at least you can be a spiritual blessing to those around you by your cheerful interest in them and their affairs.

Each of us deeply wants to make a mark, to be remembered, to leave our world a little better for having been in it. At times this act of "retirement" makes us realize with a kind of desperation that we haven't done so. Remember Grandma Moses and don't give up! You can still have a garden that people bring their visitors across town to see. You may find you can write well enough to be published, or paint well enough to be hung! You may already have started a collection that will become valuable and famous. You may be such a delight to know—cookies? stories? pert humor?—that people will make a beaten path to your door, not because you've made a better mousetrap but because you *are* one, cheese and all!

Death

The iciest plunge of all to a great number of people, even in middle age, is the thought of death and the debilitating illnesses that occasionally precede it. They evade the words dying, death, dead, and replace them by phrases such as "passing on," "gone on," "through the door," and so on. But death is a fact, as certain and natural a part of life as being born. This fact should be recognized and the proper words used even around children. Children should not be allowed to face their first heartbreaking loss of a pet, a playmate, a parent with no preparation and no immediate help.

If, because the loss is yours too, and you fear you cannot muster the strength to talk about it without breaking down, do not worry. Grief will not be more than a child can bear, if shared with a person he loves. Being shut away is much more damaging. If this seems impossible at the moment, put the child in the hands of someone else he loves—but do not shut him out of your own grief any longer than you must. Make him feel that you need him. Do not use the expressions "God took him," or "wanted him." Death does not come as a lightning stroke from God's hand, but as the result of natural law. Do not say, "God needs him"—which is probably not true! It might be possible to say, "Granny was very ill and needs to rest. God made us so that this can happen." These are my ways of dealing with children *I* love. They may not be yours. Only be sure that you do not say to a child or young person what you do not believe. If you think that death ends everything, say so. But add, "Other people believe thus and thus."

Your attitude toward death and a possible hereafter is a part of your core values for life. Roughly, people can be divided into groups of those who believe that death ends all, those who accept the teachings about death and life after death in any of the living religions, and those who are frankly agnostic at this point. Many faiths include elaborate systems of punishment and reward for sins and virtues; some hold that there are further eras of testing and training before we attain eventual happiness; some that by the goodness, the prayers, the sacrifice of others (as by Christ's crucifixion) we are brought to an eternity with God.

Some people are sure they know every detail of God's intent and of his dwelling place. Some believe that the "spirit" leaves the body forever at death, others that the spirit and body will someday be reunited. There are people who accept reincarnation as a kind of reward or punishment for their deeds in life. Others are sure that good people do not die at all, but are "translated" into the presence of gods or of others like themselves and can return to earth if needed. None of these varied points of view can be proven beyond doubt. Many, and I am one, simply believe in God and trust him without further speculation. This hodgepodge need not all be shared with children. Share your own faith; tell them that everyone does not agree with you, and that you expect that their own satisfactory conclusions must come from becoming acquainted with the beliefs of people they love and admire, from study, and from experience.

If you are afraid of death, straighten yourself out by any available means but never share that fear with youth if you can possibly help it. Talk to and read the conclusions of wise and good people. Any doctor or minister will tell you that very seldom is death agonizing, even when it results from a serious illness. Accept the fact of transience, of death, and you will be able to end your days in peace and serenity. A German writer, A. L. Vischer says in his book *On Growing Old* that a proper motto for aging is "be a good loser. . . . It is only a poor sportsman who will abuse or insult a successful opponent, protest against the verdict, explain away his defeat as being due to all manner of external circumstances and finish up by going into a sulk."

Actually, many of the very old people I have known are no longer afraid of death. They are much more afraid of losing those they love, or of living too long. They are also afraid of being no longer helpful, of becoming more and more dependent upon others, of having physical handicaps and pain, of experiencing loneliness. It seems to be more difficult to be a "good loser" about such circumstances than about the facing of death itself. But somehow we must learn to do so or we shall be more of a burden to ourselves and others than our infirmities demand.

It is good to have a supporting faith in dealing with such infirmities and in facing the fact of our own death or that of someone we love. Whatever the details of that faith, the strength and comfort it can bring is very great and should be absorbed to the utmost. Such a faith can be found clearly and repeatedly in the Bible, as in the Gospel of John, chapter 14, which has often brought comfort and strength to me and mine.

At times we find a touch of humor that lightens our seriousness about death.

A five-year-old, after attending the funeral of one grandmother, rode back to his home with the other one. He was so quiet, his much loved "granny" thought she had better ask him what he was thinking about. The conversation ran as follows:

"Is Grandmother Wallace with God now, Granny?"

"Yes, Teddy, we believe she is, as many old people are."

"Are you old, too, Granny?"

"Yes, Teddy—a little older than Grandmother Wallace."

"My goodness, Granny—do you s'pose God's forgotten about you?"

We are fortunate if we are sure he has not—in this life or the next.

PART III *It's Never Too Late*

There are wide varieties in the conditions of life for those who live to be sixty-five or older. They appear in finances, health, living conditions, length of life, and many other areas. According to our statistics, most men and women for the first five or ten years after retirement are reasonably well and more or less happily established in homes of their own. If not, the fault is generally not their age. They may have lived below the poverty level all of their lives, or perhaps they are physically handicapped in some way. They may be the products of broken homes, their own or that of their parents. Their education or training for self-support may have been inadequate. The men and women who come under such categories constitute a social problem that concerns us all. Conditions such as these that cause them to become increasingly dependent during aging must be changed primarily at their point of origin. Meanwhile they need, deserve, and must have our concern and care.

The remainder of us, if we are facing unexpected difficulties, are apt to be in other categories:

1. We may refuse to adjust to inevitable changes, and so become very difficult to plan for or live with.

2. We may have a reduction of real income through losses that we could not foresee: business failures, inflation, etc.

3. A very long life may leave us without close relatives on whom we counted for affectionate care.

4. We may become physically incapacitated at an earlier age than we had expected.

On the other hand we may be among the fortunate ones who are reasonably well, adequately supplied with our own income, usefully occupied, and much loved to the end of life. Any or all of these blessings can make life worthwhile. To achieve these conditions to whatever degree is possible must be the goal of the aging and of those who care for them. Since it is not at all unusual in our time for men and women to live into the eighties and nineties it is obviously out of the question for most of us to fully attain that goal. However, we must find ways to make these latter years rewarding for those who live them as well as for those who may become in some degree responsible for them.

A. L. Vischer's *On Growing Old* expresses what may happen in this way:

"To prove our worth in old age is a very difficult task indeed. Now we find out what we are really like; we find out whether our insights have been deep enough and our self-discipline strong enough to teach us humility and to enable us to renounce the approbation of our fellow-men. When we have reached this point, then we may breathe a sigh of relief, then a sense of inner peace . . . may enter into us and permeate our being. This much abused and so greatly feared old age may yet become our good friend. If it does, then we shall come to know the profound truth contained in the words of the old poetess, Marie von Ebner Eschenbach: 'To be humble is to be invulnerable.' "

It is not in the least necessary for our later years to be all downhill emotionally. Our physical stamina may lessen, even desert us altogether. But consider these words by J. Klasi as quoted by Vischer: "Health is the ability to endure even illness and infirmity, if not with joy and gratitude, then at least with equanimity, with dignity and with profit."

And Wilfred Monod, the French theologian and philosopher, tells us that "the soul is the body's ability to say 'nevertheless.' " At a very advanced age we still have and can use rich "gifts of the spirit," such as knowledge and wisdom, experience and reason, goodness and charm.

Have you been doing your "homework" for yourselves and with your children up to this crucial time of life? Remember, it's never too late. You can change quite a few things about yourself and your circumstances in the next five or ten years if you really want to!

As you look back, you may feel that your life has been uneventful, unimportant. Actually you have been living through very exciting years, during which you have been a part of creation, of history, of ongoing life. You may even have found answers—satisfactory to yourself—to some of the great questions men have been asking through the ages!

Chapter 6 RETROSPECTION

Realistically, you are now aware that life is approaching an end. However, as long as your name has not appeared in the "obits" there is no reason why your life should not be rich, full, and useful. You are still quite capable of wielding considerable personal influence. You may even make some definite marks on your world, though its boundaries be small. Retrospection is the mood or act of recollecting past events. You, as an aging person, are supposed to be very good at this, better than you are at remembering what happened yesterday. So make a virtue of necessity; what you remember may be of very real service to you, to those around you, and even to your world.

Suppose you begin that retrospection with the larger world, that part of life most of us expect to give up as we approach old age. It is to be hoped that since your own activities have lessened you have learned to be an interested observer of those of others, that you have kept a keen interest in the affairs of the world about you. Experience has no doubt taught you to be realistic in your understanding of life's sad and ugly phases and to hold in remembrance those that existed in your own youth. But these negative memories should not blind you to the many signs of progress, nor prevent you from hoping for more—yes, even to having a part in creating them.

You Are a Part of History

If you are my age or older you have lived through three quarters of a century crowded with excitement. You are a part of history—the kind you studied in school! My mother was in some degree involved in six wars in which our country participated; she was born only six years after the Civil War ended, and she lived to see us in Vietnam. A record of the changes in social attitudes and in world relationships, the discoveries and inventions made during her lifetime would fill a large volume. She, like the rest of us, took most of this quite calmly, without much appreciation of the tremendous importance and effect of each separate event. Many of the individual lives lived during that same period have been as dramatic as anything to be seen on stage or screen. Not all of it was good. Some of the events in your own place in history may have brought you pain and anguish. But you *lived*—through great events, and are still doing so. Count that as gain.

Because you are a part of history you can bring a calm and ordered judgment to the affairs of today. War and rumors of wars, riots and strikes, scandals in personal lives and in government are not new. There are simply more people to be involved in them, more types of communication to bring them quickly and vividly before us. It is very difficult in these days not to feel that our country is falling apart at the seams! But even the events in Chicago in 1968 had parallels in the 1920's. I was in school there then and helped in the work of a neighborhood house in a slum area pervaded by gangsters. Murders were common; street gangs existed; all of the evils of a deprived section of the community were in sight. I knew children who had never seen a living tree or growing grass, nor had they been to the lake which was within walking distance or at the end of a 5¢ streetcar ride.

Even though we have not succeeded in eliminating our current versions of such evils, we could make quite a long list of improvements. We have seen many gains for the labor force such as shorter working hours, safety rules, pensions, and Social Security. Recreational and cultural opportunities for all are increasing fast. We are seeing the gradual recognition of the inadequacy of commonly used ways to escape frustration. In our personal lives, these include heavy smoking and drinking, giving large amounts of time to tasteless and useless amusements, the use of drugs, a rampant and misdirected sexuality. In our common life they appear as the pollution and waste of our natural resources, the piling up of fortunes we do not need, guilt directed toward scapegoats, power-hunger resulting in all kinds of corruption and violence. As our present life is organized wealth, social position, political and cultural influence are in the hands of those of us who are older. It is exciting to think of what might happen if we could find a way to share that power with young idealists, together seeking more positive ways to deal with our frustrations; to have youth turn to us as comrades in arms instead of as "the enemy." Meanwhile we can assure them that many evils *can* be overcome. We have seen this happen, again and again—and often through the initiative of a single individual or a small group. Perhaps we have even helped in some such process.

Our greatest hope for positive change lies in the recognition of the importance of education. Deprived persons, minority groups, and underdeveloped nations know that lack of well-educated leaders and followers is the real root of their difficulties. Quality education and enough of it, both for earning a living and enriching a life, is as necessary as good food, housing, and health care. It is not our purpose here to define quality education except to suggest a more careful balance than we have sometimes had between academic studies, vocational training, and actual experience. We have fortunately accepted the fact that such education need not be crowded into a dozen or so early years but can be continued throughout life. So keep at it yourself, you who are aging in body but who can be very much alive in mind. Use your influence and your votes to see that everyone has an opportunity for the most and the best education possible, instead of dragging your heels when a bond issue is needed. If you have aroused in your own children an interest in and desire for a life of continuous learning you have done your country a real service.

You Are a Part of Creation

In Genesis 1:27–28 we are told that the God whom many of us know as the Creator gave to man and his helpmate "dominion" over all created things. Evidently he expected man to become a partner in the process of creation. Some children I once knew interpreted the word "dominion" by saying that "God gave us everything he had created *to use and to care for.*" In your life you have been a part of the creative process. You have borne children, planted fields and gardens, discovered uses for the metals hidden in the earth, recorded your feelings and experiences in graphic and performing arts, entered into worship, shared your learning with new generations, built governmental systems, struggled in them for freedom and a just distribution of the fruits of the earth. You have even flown to the moon and have an interested eye on the rest of the universe.

Whether man believes natural law was established by a supreme being is beside the point. Great wisdom is required to avoid the harm that results from breaking natural law. For instance, there is the breakdown of a delicate balance in wildlife when a species is destroyed; erosion follows wrong use of the earth; pollution results from reckless disposal of wastes. We have lived through floods and dust bowls and forest fires. As we see such waste going on we can still help to do something about it. We may know some legislators personally; we may even *be* one! We can write letters to those who represent us as they vote on crucial bills. We may even have stock-voting power in a company which is causing ecological troubles. Even as we recognize our mistakes we can find joy for ourselves and our families in the vast spaces that are being held in trust for outdoor recreation, in the preservation of natural beauty that adds so much to travel enjoyment, in outdoor adventures that are exciting but safe.

Having dominion over the earth begins with enjoying it— its sights and sounds, its fragrances and textures. If your present world is limited to one room, books and magazines, television and radio can help you to recall all kinds of beauty that you have seen in other days or that you have only heard about or read of. One window in your room can provide endless experiences of beauty and interest. There may be an ant on your windowsill carrying a crumb far larger than he is or a bird learning to trust you enough to use the food and water tray you fill for him each day. You can see trees and children, clouds that constantly change formation, a many-colored dawn or sunset sky, a golden sliver of new moon. You can hear and feel the wind and rain. Try to recapture the wonder a child feels for the world he is discovering through his senses. If there is such a child in your household he will bring his findings to you if you really want him to.

You Have Found Answers to Great Questions

Learning may be merely academic, but wisdom comes only when learning is in balance with rich experience. As events, personal or otherwise, go swiftly by we ask questions, ponder reasons, even say prayers which at times seem to get no replies. Such questioning occurs when we are blocked from attaining a worthwhile goal, lose someone dear to us, or see evil have its way. Not all of these puzzles have been or will be solved. You will die with many "puzzlements" still plaguing you. But as you grow very old you will find enough questions answered, enough reasons evident to make you willing to accept the fact that probably the lack of answers to the others has been due to your own faulty understanding. My own most serious questions centered about one very painful illness, the death early in life of someone dear to me, and the sad "petering out" of a good and useful life. I had answers to the first two quite soon. I am sure that in time and with trust I will have an answer to the third.

It is apparent that goodness exempts no one from the action of natural law. Nor does it exempt the good person from suffering because of the evil deeds of others. But I have known many people who were truly happy in spite of adverse circumstances, even circumstances caused by the malice of others. Everyone you will ever know, no matter how young or how old, is asking the same questions, seeking answers to the same puzzling and disturbing facts of life. Now is the time to share the answers you have found. Keep the doors open. Be ready to listen patiently, with love and compassion. Keep the confidences given you. Be direct and honest if you have a bit of wisdom to give, but leave the listener free to make his own choices, his own decisions. If you can do all this you will probably be the most popular person around. You may even need a secretary for appointments!

So you have been looking backward. Would you like to live your life over again? certain parts of it? Do you feel a sense of satisfaction as you look back? regret? cynicism? sorrow? Can you be objective enough about your life to face it honestly? Most of all, have you become what Dr. Vischer calls a good loser—one who can put aside useless regret, bitterness, self-pity and accept life as it has been and is? Have you wiped out all the "signs of senility" that lessen your attractiveness to others? Have you attained a detachment from sound and fury, a gentle sense of humor, a serenity and compassion that draws people to you more and more?

If so, the time given to retrospection, while no doubt revealing a number of old wounds, will be healing rather than hurting.

Chapter 7 INDEPENDENCE

Independence is largely a matter of finances and health. As our statistics inform us, there are growing numbers of aging people who are able to live without depending upon any outside assistance. The success of such living is the result of careful planning and common sense. In the twenty years beyond the customary job retirement age of sixty-five certain realities must be faced. Much depends on what has been done through middle age to guard health and build reserves of income and to develop sound attitudes toward aging.

There are, of course, no fixed schedules of "happenings." In general, people in their seventies become (allowing for individual temperament) pessimistic, with a negative attitude toward aging, illness, and death. They are frequently irritable, self-pitying. But once past eighty, there is a pride in age, a comfortable faith in life, stability that is tranquil and serene. There is an increasing invulnerability to illness or accident. Earlier in life similar plateaus were evident. Forty to seventy is normally marked by a sedate and settled maturity, with occasional crises from forty to fifty. Just before retirement there is a brief period of anxiety during which the aging person is more concerned with self than others.

Unless he has become senile or ill, an aging person's mind is capable of being quite active. The characteristics of age should be acquired wisdom, willingness to listen, interest in change, and response to new ideas. But do not expect too much. Remember that you are dealing with a lifetime of thought patterns, habits, attitudes, and they can be rather sturdy!

Men and women who are aging need to be taken seriously as persons. As with very young children, they should be given every possible opportunity to make decisions and choices no matter how minor these may be. As they become infirm, their own interest in making decisions will weaken, but encourage them to do so, especially those which concern their own welfare. If there are major family decisions to make concerning a change in their way of life or if there is concern about the state of their health, bring them into the discussion at some point, preferably doing so with that member of the family with whom they will talk freely and to whom they will reveal any fears or anxieties they may be having about aging, illness, or death. Then perhaps the whole family can face the facts together. Here is a place where old and trusted friends, or your present rabbi, priest, or minister—if close to you—can help.

Whether independent or dependent there are these general needs for the aging:

1. Good health, to the extent possible
2. Financial security
3. Comfort
4. Appropriate and satisfactory living arrangements
5. Companionship and affection
6. Interpersonal relationships, if possible across age groups
7. Varied occupations, creative activities
8. Continued usefulness, being needed in some way
9. A settled life philosophy
10. A sound faith and close relationship with its organized form (as church or synagogue).

A Place to Live

One major concern is the provision for satisfactory living quarters. As has been mentioned, a large proportion of our very old people are still living as couples in their own homes, with a varying degree of financial independence. This is the way most of them prefer to live. Men frequently continue to do so after losing their wives; they often marry again at an advanced age. Women too remain independent or marry again after being widowed. A larger proportion of women however make a new home with a relative, usually a son or daughter.

If it is at all possible, responsible relatives should insist upon and help all older folk to maintain such independence. Sons and daughters can join in providing finances necessary for parents to continue to live as they always have or for a move to one of the many attractive retirement centers for older people throughout the country. These vary from cottages in residential areas to high-rise apartments in the heart of a city. An increasing number of them include many forms of recreation and health services.

A growing trend, if you expect at some time to be responsible for an elderly person, is to build, as part of your own home, a guest wing or separate guest house. This can eventually become semi-independent living quarters for such a person. Such a procedure can of course be reversed. A couple wishing to give up the burdens of a large home can turn it over to a younger member of the family or rent it, having provided such a guest house or wing for themselves.

When the time comes that you are living with or very near relatives remember that you will need vacations from each other, so plan for this. Some elderly people love sentimental journeys to places and people dear to them; others prefer something new and exciting. It is not necessary to travel a great distance to find a change of scene. Interesting new developments also make it possible to get about more easily in one's own town or neighborhood, such as a small, electrically driven cart or adult tricycle. Motorized wheel chairs are also available. A change of companionship is also a possibility; the large family goes on vacation and a much enjoyed guest shares the quarters of the elderly housebound relative. Even if travel must be reduced to the level of TV, radio, movies, a slide viewer or a picture album, any or all of these can give a feeling of movement, of change.

Experience has taught us much about independent living for the aging. However it is well to remember that as our reactions become slower, our sight, hearing, and balance less dependable, there are ways to make life easier, no matter what the type of housing.

For the mobile person
   Living quarters on one floor
   Labor saving appliances
   Storage space for personal treasures
      (easily accessible)
   A small yard or patio
   Church, stores, and sources of recreation nearby

For the housebound (and mobile)
   Automatic heat
   Non-slip floors and bathroom surfaces, with
      safety rails and handgrips
   Good lighting, including lighted switches
   Access to a sunny spot
   Open shelves that can be reached without
      bending or climbing.

This list can be expanded as necessary. For instance, a smooth tile instead of carpets is preferable if a wheelchair or other hospital equipment must be used. Such equipment is easier to move if it has large rather than small wheels and all wheels should be lockable. Good equipment can be rented or purchased with the help of many types of insurance and Medicare. Whether the aging live alone or with other people, such details make life easier and safer.

If an elderly person is living in smaller quarters than before, a feeling of space can be achieved by: soft, light colors; simple furniture and lack of clutter; hangings, upholstery, and carpets in plain colors or very small patterns; mirrors for depth.

Something To Do

Besides a proper place to live and some adjustments in your way of living, "something to do" is a necessity. As long as a person is reasonably active, light housekeeping, entertaining guests, hobbies, outdoor activities and so on are both possible and wise. If you are staying where you have always lived this will be no problem—more "things to do" than you can manage will come your way. One very good thing to do is to keep up your interest in local, national, and world affairs. My mother watched and listened to political speeches on TV preceding each election and voted—at least for national candidates—until 1968 when the election came during her last illness. As she had been in a wheelchair for twelve years this meant making necessary arrangements and some difficulties, such as crowding her, the wheelchair, me, and the official "helper" into a voting booth. She chose her own candidates and her choice was not always that of her family!

Keep working as long as possible at anything you have

learned to do, especially if you enjoy the activity and do it well. My town is rich in creative workers—craftsmen, artists, writers, A large proportion of them are over fifty years of age, many are seventy or more. Do you play an instrument and know some lovely old folk songs, such as are currently popular? Play them, sing them. Do you crochet or knit or sew? Make things. One of my most cherished possessions is an afghan my grandmother knit after she was eighty and blind. The oldest person I ever saw was at the moment crocheting a baby jacket for an expected great-grandchild. She was 104—and did not need glasses. Many an older person who has not even planned for a vocation for his latter years has suddenly found himself with an earning capacity he had never dreamed of: in art (as Grandma Moses), in drama (character parts), in skilled crafts of all kinds. My favorite set of costume jewelry was made of American jade by a rock hound who was nearly ninety. Now living in a retirement center, this delightful gentleman recently made a pin as a birthday gift for a friend and told her, "Now tell 'em it was made when I was ninety-five."

There is literally no limit to the number of activities available even to those who must increasingly save their strength. Those with limited strength or mobility may be able to enjoy such activities as photography, bird-watching, or sculpture. As for the many elderly folk who are well and active there are endless types of community, church, social, and business opportunities still open that do not demand too much of their time and energy. Also organizations such as the American Association of Retired Persons provide local companionship, creative activities, and guided travel tours for the relatively independent. Some of them even make possible life and car insurance beyond that available from commercial firms!

Achievement

Older people are not necessarily restricted to a passive role in life. The labor force of those over sixty-five has dropped from 80.6 percent in 1870 to something near 41 percent. This burdens the young and takes away a basic right of age, that of sharing their minds and skills. Retirement age is firmly established now by the pension plan rules of business, unions, and corporations, and by the Social Security laws. But there have always been men and women who continue to "labor" even after retirement age. For instance, one man I know who was an auditor helped out for many years (into his early nineties) at "peak load" times in his local post office or in county or federal tax systems; another at the same age continues to help his friends fill out tax forms. One of my favorite couples, at ages seventy-six and eighty-four, are ready to go anywhere in the world at the drop of a hat and until recently have been actively connected with major archaeological "digs" and guided travel tours. They are a part of every worthwhile project in church and community, and no one could be better company.

In one of our eastern states a doctor who has passed his one hundredth birthday is still "consultant emeritus" for the local hospital. He gave up his last patient at the age of ninety-seven, after a long life of varied medical service. At the same time he turned in his driver's license! A much loved legend in his community, he is known for his warmth and wit, vigor and love of life. A surprise gift for his birthday was a year's subscription to Meals on Wheels, a service which supplies two well-balanced meals, one hot and one cold, to elderly people living alone.

In the Southwest, which is my home, you constantly meet men and women who were pioneers. The women are especially interesting. They are old—very old—but erect, vigorous, and often real "characters." With their husbands they came as brides to homestead ranches. Many of them lost their husbands to outlaws, Indians, or catastrophes of nature. Yet they raised their families and held their land under unbelievably difficult conditions. Some of them made sizable fortunes as farmers or in cattle, oil, or mining. Far away in the opposite corner of the country are some hale and hearty old men, who were captains and crews of the sailing ships that ranged the seas of all the world, and who still go out with our fishing fleets. They have exciting stories to tell and a salty humor.

Then, too, we forget that many of the great fortunes were made by men well past middle age. They had known privation for years as they stubbornly fought to fulfill their dreams—a long list of inventions, explorations, and scientific discoveries. They were not originally sparked by a desire for money, but by a demanding idea, a desire for useful achievement. We can give them credit for imagination and persistence without crowning them as saints! Some of them came to deserve the name of "robber barons," but they were strong and colorful characters as long as they lived. Many of those who headed great dynasties later instilled in their descendants a real sense of social responsibility, which issued in the public benefactions we too often take for granted. These include conservation of land, worldwide medical research, museums and art galleries, centers for the performing arts, libraries, colleges and universities. We also tend to forget that in the government we are so quick to criticize there have been, before and since the American Revolution, literally an army of wise, dedicated—and old!—men who have made us the envy of the world. These, and many others less well known, grew old the way everyone would like to and almost no one plans for.

And so we find that as long as he is relatively independent, the aging person has many options as to how he can live and what he can do. But let us be realistic. As the years go on we are constantly on the brink of some type of dependency. Can we accept help with grace or give it with affection and generosity?

Chapter 8 DEPENDENCE

Eventually it became my task to care for three elderly invalids, each one dependent upon me to some degree financially and almost totally for personal care and affection. I learned many things from them that I trust will help me to move into my own old age with a degree of understanding and grace. Some of these "learnings" are recorded here in the hope that difficult, amusing, or endearing incidents contain germs of wisdom that can be applied if you *become* dependent, or *have* a dependent as old age develops. In dependency, the person who has the responsibility must almost always take the initiative to achieve a satisfactory relationship.

As life closes in upon the very old, they need, as does a child, tender care, affection, comfortable living, and as many and varied experiences as we can supply to fill the long days and nights. Far too often we fail in all these regards, especially as they apply to the old and infirm in hospitals, institutions, and nursing homes. Just as muscles atrophy with lack of use, minds, hearts, and spirits die a slow death if they are not fed. But there must be some response on the part of those being cared for, too. Do you remember the nurse who said that as people become old and ill the nice ones get nicer and the mean ones meaner? It may be too late for any great change in those we care for, but it is never too late to make sure that *we* are in the first category!

Have you ever noticed that to most of us, "old age" is a period to which we have not yet attained, no matter what birthday we have passed? My mother, although increasingly in need of constant and almost total help, would never have recognized herself as a subject for the study of geriatrics—"a subdivision of medicine which is concerned with the diseases of the aging." You see, the arthritis and neuritis, the shocks of family crises, which brought her pain and eventually incapacity had been with her more than half of her life. She did not connect them with old age. These were illnesses and happenings common to all ages, as were high blood pressure, heart attacks, and other organic mishaps.

Mother would also have failed to see herself as a subject for the study of gerontology, "the investigation of the phenomena of old age." Birth and growth; the joys and sorrows of childhood, adolescence, and married life; the aging and death of contemporaries were accepted as parts of any normal life. They were to be dealt with as best you knew how. If any situation got beyond your capacities, you received help from relatives and friends, just as you had often given help to them, or from your church and other such organizations, because that is a part of *what they are for.* As her ability to function gradually lessened, I think we too, while saddened by it, accepted this as a normal condition in a very long life. We hoped that at some future time science would make it possible to live comfortably as well as long.

Public Dependency

The hardest dependency to accept is that which involves public sources. This includes any type of public institution, such as nursing homes, hospitals, homes for the aged, home health service—any care that is given by strangers. If such care is necessary, try to think of it or explain it as a just due to an aged person who has been as good a citizen as possible. If such care is being given to a person you love or are in some degree responsible for, check carefully on its quality. Also provide the small attentions by mail or personal visits that will help make the situation bearable. Such attentions are important even if the aging person or his family can pay for excellent care in a private institution. It is a bitter experience to find it necessary to explain the indifference or neglect of one's family to contemporaries. Their attentions, on the other hand, are a matter for pride. There are many instances of aging men or women in such situations inventing visits, gifts, letters to boast of, when a real loving concern does not exist.

Family Dependency

Becoming increasingly dependent, financially or for personal care, upon relatives is not easy for any of those concerned. Plans should be made well in advance of need. There must be an investigation of all possible alternatives and much objective consultation, to make sure that responsibility is fairly shared within a family and that the happiest solution for the person to be cared for is found. The excellent books listed in the bibliography explain various types of help available for the aging. But as this field is constantly expanding be sure you have the latest local, state, and federal information.

Childlikeness

As advanced age comes on, and possibly with it debilitating illness, an interesting change is often noted. Physically and emotionally the elderly person reverts to early childhood. He is not necessarily *childish* but *childlike*. This goes so far as a childlike desire for a safe, cozy nest; of concentrating on his own needs and desires and responding most fully to those who meet them. As do very young children, very old people need a lot of love.

Perhaps this return to childhood is why older people remember with such clarity the events and persons of their younger days, but forget so quickly the ones of recent years. At ninety-five and ninety-six my mother occasionally called "Mama!" when she wanted attention. One night, after her arm and side had been burned with hot coffee she cried quietly and said, "I want my mother!" If we can see that such persons have a few pictures, objects, furnishings that they connect with younger and happier days, and someone to talk with them occasionally about those days, this yearning may be somewhat assuaged.

Sorrow

Mother was not apt to pity herself or ask for pity. However, shortly after the wife of her youngest brother died (preceded by all of her brothers, sisters and inlaws) she wept in the night saying over and over, "They're all gone but me!" Surely the many points at which the very old can feel such utter desolation call for all the compassion and comfort our hearts can give. This sadness also comes to them when younger members of the family die and the feeling of living beyond one's time, of uselessness, of taking the place of someone who is needed, is intensified. As with children, do not encourage fantasy about death or an unwillingness to face reality. Try to see yourself and help the elderly to see themselves as links in a chain in family and society, with a responsibility to keep the chain strong. If the older person professes a faith, remind him that such faith brings not extinction but fulfillment, for himself and others. If we have such trust or knowledge, the details of fulfillment do not seem necessary.

Mother—along with most of the very old people I have

known—was able to accept personal hardships with, as Klasi says, "equanimity and dignity." With Mother, this was because she had always been surrounded by a warm heritage of family love, by affection, concern, goodwill. Very young children also learn to love by being loved—and so are unable to imagine a lack of it anywhere. At every stage of life we give respect, compassion, love because it has been given to us, by someone, sometime, somewhere. This is as important at life's end as at its beginning, for both giver and receiver. On the whole, however, the aged are more apt to be emotionally mature than their children and grandchildren. Most of them have come to terms with life and have developed a tough emotional fiber.

Religion

One's faith, beliefs, or religion can be a very strengthening factor as old age comes upon us. Do all that you can to keep an older person in contact with such faith and with its organized program, such as a church or synagogue. Every kind of organized religion should keep closely in touch with its older followers, especially as they become housebound. If the church that means most to your invalid neglects this, remind the pastor of how much pleasure some attention would bring. Most of all, personal calls by rabbi, priest, or minister are appreciated. Also other callers, religious reading matter, flowers or plants, and other small gifts can be meaningful. In family or personal worship the literature of a common faith, *shared with someone,* is helpful.

Communication

Aging people who do not get about much should be encouraged to talk by carrying on conversations with those around them as frequently as possible. They can very easily fall into a state of lethargy. Often they can be led to continue reading also, by giving them easily handled magnifying glasses and a holder for books, magazines, or papers. Reduce the extent of reading matter and the length of conversations as time goes on. Communication does not necessarily get more difficult with great age, but it *can*—and to me this was the saddest part of Mother's last years. I wasn't sure whether she *couldn't or wouldn't* as she practically stopped talking. Once I cried out to her rather desperately, "Mother, *can't* you talk to me?" A slow shake of the head was the only answer, but even that meant she could *hear* and *understand*. It was enough to make the apparently futile effort of talking to her worthwhile.

Continuing Hobbies

Older people, mobile or not, can be helped to continue a former interest or hobby. One delightful old lady I know had both legs amputated as a result of diabetes and soon afterward her husband died in an automobile accident. Surely this was enough to make almost anyone give up. But her family made it possible for her to have a sunny space in her room to grow a beautiful collection of African violets to which everyone who knew her constantly added. There were also gifts of gardening tools, plant foods, and equipment to give her plants the right amounts of light, air, and water. She made a virtue of the necessity of exercising her fingers by using them to do clerical work for the Boy Scouts and to knit baby afghans for a nearby hospital.

An elderly man who was shut away from the outdoor life he loved found that a bit of woodland within sight of his window was the home of a variety of small animals and birds. A powerful field glass increased his range of sight; one of his grandsons became a fascinated partner in these activities. He provided food and water to bring their small friends closer to the window and later took pictures of them to study together and share with their friends. This same "old" man built a new friendship with his son-in-law (the man of the house) by teaching him to make fishing flies.

Little Things

It takes very little, really, to please and interest the very old or infirm. The important thing is to put variety and life into hours that can be very long and dull. Experiment a bit to discover what seems to bring pleasure, even if you do not get much response in words. Use your imagination to inject a few surprises into what can become monotonous routine. Some of the special enjoyments in their lives are guests, family celebrations, food, anything that adds movement or sound to their day (as, a view of a busy street, television, good-looking clothes, their own treasures, little children). Supply these in many attractive ways. Most of all, try a frequent change of location. Even a move to the next room or a bed in a different position will help.

There must be at least some one person on whom the aged person is emotionally dependent, in whose love he trusts. This becomes most necessary at points where there are difficult decisions to make or orders that must be obeyed. For with an elderly person—especially if they are ill—there are times when it is imperative, as with a young child, to say fimly, "You must!" There are limits that cannot be passed, risks that dare not be taken, regulations that must be obeyed, treatments that have to be given.

Once upon a time I was given a most helpful recipe for successful human relations under any conditions. I have found it to be deeply true.

"If you love anyone enough you can say anything to them

that needs to be said; if you don't, you deserve what you get if you try."

And love is the only thing that can take the sting out of dependency on both sides!

Chapter 9 *REWARD*

Recently I heard of a young man who in talking of his family, said with considerable pride, "My grandfather's about ninety and kind of ornery!"

The greatest reward that can come to youth, middle age, or old age is an absence of any generation gap, up or down. In our earlier pioneer days, there was a natural closeness between age groups. On farms, in small towns and places of business, in a less specialized world, very young and very old people were needed. They had real and important jobs to do, to help the responsible middle agers. No one had any reason to feel left out.

Nor did anyone feel under a burdensome authority. Younger members of a family knew there were limits to their freedom, largely concerned with an avoidance of areas of danger. Within those limits there was a great deal of room for independent choice, action, experiment. Very old people had clearly turned over their heavier responsibilities to the next generation, but their place in the scheme of things was still a good one. Their experience and wisdom were welcomed. Their oversight of the household and of younger children freed those now in control for more important tasks. These oldsters were still very much a part of family and community life.

All ages and stages touched at many points—which was the

important life principle. Children went together to the same school building—even to the same room. Everyone went together to church, barn raisings and picnics, camp meetings and dances, celebrations both personal and patriotic, from the youngest baby to the oldest great-aunt.

But we would not go back to those days if we could. Life was not all roses! We would not, for instance, go back to the one-room school, for many good reasons. However, after a long time and many failures we have discovered that *people* cannot effectively be put into *any* rigid groupings to be educated, whether by age, reading ability, or IQ's! There is clearly a remarkable educative experience in a mixture of ages, kinds, and colors of people.

We should have known this. It is probably the one thing that gives the American dream its rightness in spite of all that goes wrong. Put a group of people of varied ages, backgrounds, goals, and abilities together to work and play in security and freedom and what happens? Not always continual peace, but an attainment of balance, a process of learning and growth, a rubbing off of sharp edges, and better decisions in the long run than those at which an intellectual aristocracy arrives. Slowly but surely mutual respect and responsibility emerges. For unity in diversity seems to be inherently a way to successful human relationships and in them great rewards.

Rewards for Youth

There are certain rewards that come in youth, middle age, and old age in good family life. In youth the chief advantage is in free and comfortable access to adults of all ages and many kinds. For instance, such access broadens the base of youth's feeling of security, which no longer depends entirely on their parents. Then too, it adds variety and richness to their experiences and so improves the building of value systems. The initiative in such comradeship must come from adults through their friendly interest in the affairs of youth. Young people are not always at ease with their elders. They are afraid of covert amusement, violation of confidences, and conversational taboos.

In turn, it is rewarding to adults to *live with* youth. This does not mean that they must talk youth's language, strive for their appearance, or share their recreation. It simply means to be on hand when needed. There is a poplar song that says, "People who need people are the luckiest people in the world." This is true and it works in every direction. We must by experimenting discover what are the right times and places to be available. Sometimes it is just a matter of saying the right words in the right tone, not like a judge pronouncing a sentence! As . . .

"Tell me about . . ."

"I'm curious. May I ask you . . .?"

The gift of age to youth can be this kind of openness, of readiness to listen, of—yes—a change of viewpoint. In return, youth's gift to age is renewal. For suddenly you remember some long-ago points at which you felt lost, and terribly young, and *not listened to*. You have touched each other's lives in mutual understanding in spite of the generation gap.

Rewards for the Middle-Aged

Rewards for you who are the harried middle-aged can be as great as your responsibilities. They come from three directions—from your contemporaries, from youth, and from the aged. No doubt by this time you have extended your friendships, done reasonably well in your work, made a place for yourself in the community. You have deepened your relationship with husband or wife far beyond the initial impetus of desire and romantic love.

You have proudly watched your children grow to be responsible adults, with whom you can talk as friends. They are dealing with a new generation of children in ways they remember with affection and gratitude as yours—even to exact gestures and words. And—also a reward—you have ceased to fear age, as you allowed yourself to really enjoy older people, whether independent or dependent. You can view both youth and age with appreciation, humor, and tenderness, because of the willing and loving response you have made to their need. Now, serene and courageous, alert and open-minded, interested and interesting you are ready for the last great adventure no matter how or when it comes.

There is another type of reward—delayed rather than instant —that comes to the middle-aged and aging. This lies in the discovery that you have deeply touched another life for good. Parents and teachers are most apt to have this kind of reward. One of your grown-up children says to you—a bit hesitantly,

"Do you know what I'll always remember about you? Well . . ."

Rewards for the Aged

We have given testimony to the fact that growing old can be just as good—or as bad—as any other stage of life.

In *A Gift of Joy* Helen Hayes tells of a conversation with a neighbor of her hostess in Cuernavaca, Mexico. He came across the garden to tell them he had decided the evening air was too chilly to join them in a projected picnic. At eighty his "gait was somewhat slow, and his shoulders stooped just a tiny bit. His silver-white hair contrasted attractively with his bronzed Mayan face. . . .

". . . he remarked that . . . one of the pleasures of old age was that he didn't have to go anywhere he didn't want to. 'The last fifteen years have been the happiest and most serene of my life,' he said. 'Old age is wonderful. . . . I do as I please, read when I please. Of course, I have my frailties. I couldn't run down the street. But the compensations more than make up for that. You're too young to understand,' he concluded with a mischievous smile.

"Well, at sixty-five I don't consider myself a chicken exactly. But Eduardo wouldn't listen to my protestations. That seems to be another of the pleasures of age. You can be absolutely sure that you are right. And you don't care whether or not anyone else agrees with you. I haven't reached that happy state yet. But I must say that I have begun to understand what Eduardo was talking about. Certainly, Eduardo has overcome one of the great fears of life, probably the second greatest fear we have, the fear of growing old. The greatest fear is death. I don't know why we should fear our own mortality so much; I think it is too bad that death isn't accepted as part of life.

"And it's really about time that age was accepted as a part of life too. . . .

"It is a pleasure to look at the serene beauty of the faces of the aging Indian women in Mexico. . . . there is nothing more beautiful than an unadorned old face with the lines that tell a story, a story of a life that has been lived with some fullness. I don't care whether it's a life that has been lived in goodness or in mischief, if it has been lived fully there is an interesting and arresting quality in that face—in those lines that life has written there."

The greatest rewards come to you from those around you—from the ongoing family, from old and new friends of all ages, from everyone who has found you good to be with. These rewards come as you put aside frustrations and bitterness, grudges and fears. You have come to terms with life; it has done its best and worst. You can even join Christopher Morley in a bit of wry humor as you contemplate it!

ETERNITY AND THE TOOTH*

In regard to Eternity (said the Old Mandarin)
I feel about it as I do about one of my teeth.
Every now and then it gives me
A devil of a twinge,
And for a while
I groan and can think of naught else.
Then the anguish abates and I dismiss it from my mind.
But I know, just the same,
That some day
I've got to go through with it.

And won't it be exciting?

*Christopher Morley, "Eternity and the Tooth," *Translations from the Chinese* (New York: George H. Doran Company, 1922), p. 78.

⊷§BIBLIOGRAPHY

Of some one hundred books I examined or read carefully, this list includes those most usable by laymen. Those labeled "professional" are largely reports of studies made by university departments related to our subject, and are more detailed or more specialized than the others. They are, on the whole, books for use by professionals in the field of gerontology.

Part i

Call, Alice. *Toward Adulthood.* Philadelphia: Lippincott, 1964.

Carrier, Blanche. *Integrity for Tomorrow's Adults.* New York: Thomas Y. Crowell, 1959.

Fedder, Ruth. *You: The Person You Want to Be.* New York: McGraw-Hill, 1957.

Jones, Eve. *Raising Your Child in a Fatherless Home.* New York: Free Press of Glencoe, Macmillan Company, 1963.

Lally, James J. *The Over Fifty Health Manual.* Englewood Cliffs, N.J.: Prentice-Hall, 1961.

Landis, Mary and Judson. *Building Your Life.* Englewood Cliffs, N.J.: Prentice-Hall, 1964. (For youth.)

Leaf, Munro. (All for children.)
  Manners Can Be Fun. Philadelphia: Lippincott, 1958.
  Health Can Be Fun. Philadelphia: Lippincott, 1943.

How to Behave and Why. Philadelphia: Lippincott, 1946.

Russell, David H. *Children's Thinking.* Boston: Ginn & Co., 1965.

Winn, Albert C. *The Worry and Wonder of Being Human.* Richmond: The CLC Press, 1967.

PART II

Baird, Janet H. *These Harvest Years.* Garden City, N.Y.: Doubleday & Company, 1951.

Cumming, Elaine, and Henry, William H. *Growing Old: The Process of Disengagement.* New York: Basic Books, 1961. (Professional study of the psychological and social process.)

Davis, Maxine. *Get the Most Out of Your Best Years.* New York: Dial Press, 1960. (For women.)

Fried, Barbara. *The Middle-Age Crisis.* New York: Harper & Row, 1967.

Gallup, George, and Hill, Evan. *The Secrets of Long Life.* New York: Random House, 1960.

Germant, Leonard. *You're Older Than You Think.* Kalamazoo: Western Michigan University Press, 1960.

Lawton, George. *Aging Successfully.* New York: Columbia University Press, 1946.

Lewis, Adele, and Bobroff, Edith. *From Kitchen to Career.* Indianapolis: Bobbs-Merrill Company, 1965. (For women.)

Miner, C. S. *How to Get an Executive Job After 40.* New York: Macmillan Company, 1968.

Steincrohn, Peter J. *Live Longer and Enjoy It.* Englewood Cliffs, N.J.: Prentice-Hall, 1956.

Stern, Edith, and Ross, Mabel. *You and Your Aging Parents.* New York: Harper & Row, 1965.

Vischer, Adolf L. *On Growing Old.* Translated by Gerald Onn.

Boston: Houghton Mifflin, 1967.

Ware, George W. *A New Guide to Happy Retirement.* New York: Crown Publishers, 1968. (Not only about retirement but a wide range of other problems of the aging.)

PART III

Angel, Juvenal L. *Occupations for Men & Women after 45.* New York: World Trade Academy Press, 1964.

Arthur, Julietta K. *How to Help Older People.* Philadelphia: Lippincott, 1954.

Burgess, Frank Gelett. *Look Eleven Years Younger.* New York: Simon and Schuster, 1937.

Cabot, Natalie Harris. *You Can't Count on Dying.* Boston: Houghton Mifflin, 1961.

Collins, Thomas. *The Golden Years.* New York: John Day, 1956. (Mainly concerns retirement and health.)

Comfort, Alex. *The Process of Aging.* New York: New American Library, 1964.

Department of Health, Education, and Welfare:
Old Age Bibliography (1964)
Facts about Older Americans (1966), #410
A Profile of the Older American, #228
Middle-Aged and Older People in American Society, #227
Some Basic Priorities in Services for Older Americans
The above leaflets, published by the Administration on Aging, can be purchased for about 15¢ each from:
The Superintendent of Documents
U.S. Government Printing Office
Washington, D.C. 20402

Lang, Gladys Engels (ed.). *Old Age in America.* Bronx, N.Y.: H. W. Wilson, 1961.

Lehman, Harvey C. *Age and Achievement.* Princeton, N.J.: Princeton University Press, 1953. (Professional study of relation between chronological age and achievement.)

Peck, Joseph H. *Let's Rejoin the Human Race.* Englewood Cliffs, N.J.: Prentice-Hall, 1963.

Shock, Nathan W. *Trends in Gerontology.* Stanford, Calif.: Stanford University Press, 1957.

Smith, Ethel S. *The Dynamics of Aging.* New York: W. W. Norton & Co., 1956. (Includes preparing youth for aging.)

Soule, George. *Longer Life.* New York: Viking Press, 1958.

Thurber, James. *The Middle-Aged Man on the Flying Trapeze.* New York: Grosset and Dunlap, 1960.

Tibbitts, Clark. *Handbook of Social Gerontology.* Chicago: University of Chicago Press, 1960.

Walton, Sidney. *How to Make All the Money You Want While Collecting Social Security.* Profit Research, 1962.

Wassersug, Joseph D. *How to Be Healthy and Happy After Sixty.* New York: Abelard-Schuman, 1966.

Essays

Crowe, Charles M. *Getting Ready for Tomorrow.* New York: Abingdon Press, 1959.

Scott-Maxwell, Florida. *The Measure of My Days.* New York: Alfred A. Knopf, 1968.

Steincrohn, Peter J. *Forget Your Age!* Garden City, N.Y.: Doubleday & Company, 1945.

Plays

Johnson, Crane. *Past Sixty.* San Francisco: International Theatre Press, 1953. (Four one-act plays; small royalty. Address: Suite 230, 742 Market St., San Francisco, Calif.)

Historical Quotes

Tibbitts, Clark, and Donahue, Wilma. *Aging in Today's Society.* Englewood Cliffs, N.J.: Prentice-Hall, 1960. (Quotations on aging from Aristotle to Shakespeare, from Anne Lindberg to the *AFL-CIO News.*)